FISHING
The Mid-Columbia

Arnold J. Theisen

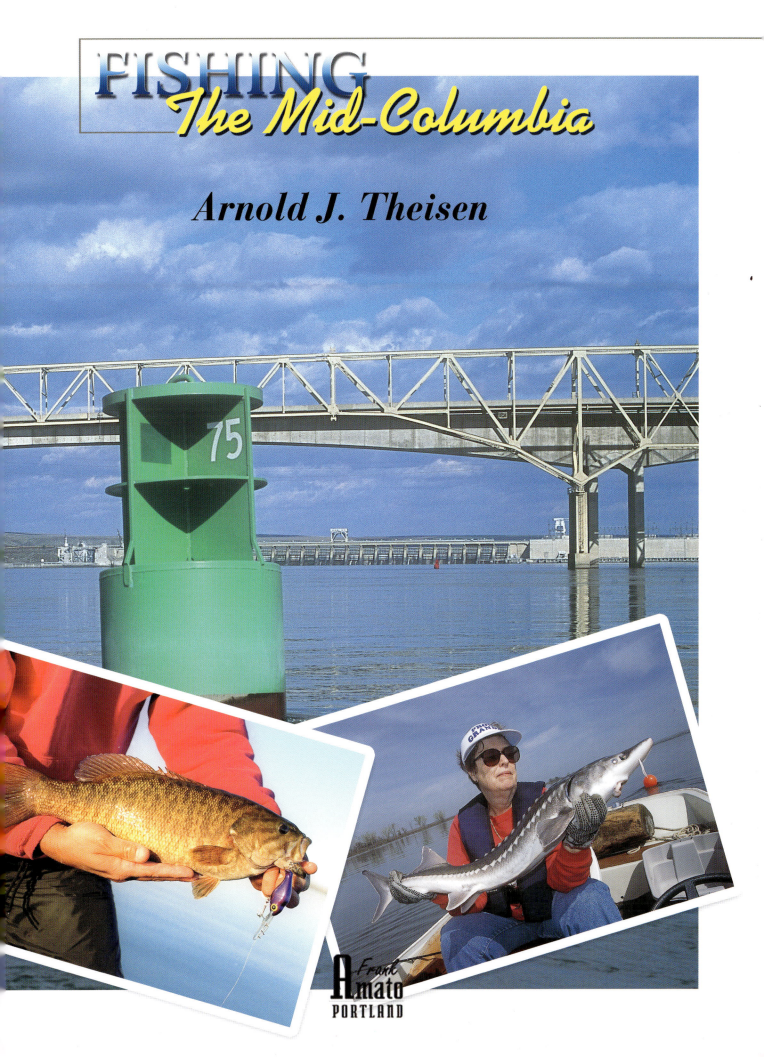

FISHING
The Mid-Columbia

Arnold J. Theisen

Frank
Amato
PORTLAND

ACKNOWLEDGEMENTS

Steve Daulton in his 20-foot Alumaweld at the Boardman Marina and RV Park.

This book is dedicated to Steve Daulton, friend and neighbor, who taught me most everything I know about fishing the Columbia River. Steve is an expert at fishing anything that swims in this river, but his specialty is walleye. Raised in Boardman and Irrigon since he was just a young lad, he was fishing walleye before walleye were cool. He talks fondly of days in the 1980s when it was common to net several fish over 10 pounds in a single outing. Over the past two decades he has acquired skill not matched by many other anglers. A frequent contestant in local walleye tournaments, Steve has earned more than his share of prizes in these competitions. He and long-time fishing partner, Travis Hyder, walked away with top honors in the 1998 High Desert Marine Walleye Derby. Daulton is one of those rare individuals who can remember every fish he ever caught; and what's better, he's perfectly willing to tell you about it. If he didn't already have a good day job he would probably be a professional fishing guide.

Garland Wright and Jack Collins also contributed significantly to my understanding of these waters. Both being retired, these veteran anglers are more likely to be found out on the river than anywhere else on any given day of the year.

Rod McKenzie has been a constant source of good information about local conditions. Besides spending a lot of time on the water, he gets valuable information by virtue of running his business, High Desert Marine, in Hermiston. Here he gets to pick the brains of the best anglers in the region who frequently stop by his store to buy or just trade stories. He always knows what's hot and what's not. His daughter, Lara Arriola, is the principal tackle buyer for the largest tackle selection in the region. If you want to know what the fish are hitting on, ask Lara. If she doesn't have it, you don't need it.

Last but not least, I am proud to acknowledge the greatest catch of my life, my Wife Eileen. Without her patience, support, and encouragement, this effort would not have been possible.

Published in 2004 by
FRANK AMATO PUBLICATIONS, INC.
PO Box 82112 • Portland, Oregon 97282 • (503) 653-8108
Softbound ISBN: 1-57188-313-4 • Softbound UPC: 0-81127-00146-0

Photography: Arnold J. Theisen
Book Design: Esther Poleo
Printed in Hong Kong

CONTENTS

PREFACE

My Philosophy

Many fishing pros subscribe to a scientific approach, utilizing an array of instruments to keep track of water temperature, depth, color, clarity, acidity (PH) level, thermocline, barometric pressure, time, air temperature, phase of the moon and other factors designed to give them a competitive edge. These factors are important to understanding the habits of fish and their propensity to bite. I don't discount any of these theories. If I depended on fishing for a living I would probably pay more attention to scientific and biological factors.

But I prefer a more pragmatic approach. I'm retired now. I fish for recreation. I don't want my recreation to feel like work. If you work a regular 40-hour week you probably fish for recreation too. The best time to go fishing, in my opinion, is anytime you can. If you go fishing whenever you can find the time, without worrying about scientific factors, my experience suggests that much of the time enough of these factors will be in your favor to permit you to catch fish. Sometimes you will get skunked. It happens to all of us, even the pros, so let's not worry about it. Why deny yourself the opportunity to fish just because the scientific factors are not all perfect? In my book there are only two rules for successful fishing: 1. Show up! 2. Get your line in the water!

WHY HERE?

The setting for much of this book is the stretch of the Columbia River that I consider to be my home waters, specifically the 39 river miles between McNary Dam and Three Mile Canyon. Why this section? Simply because these are the waters most accessible to me from my hometown of Irrigon, Oregon. I have no doubt that many of the tips and techniques described here will work on other sections of the river or even on other rivers, but I can make no specific claims about other waters that I am not familiar with.

But that's not the best reason for selecting these waters. The best reason is that these waters are rich with fishing opportunity affording an incredible variety of game fish on a year-round basis to professionals and amateurs alike. There is every reason to believe that this stretch of the Columbia River could very well yield the next world record walleye, and even if it doesn't, it still yields some of the biggest walleye this country has ever seen and it does so every year. There are white sturgeon here nearly as big as many of the boats used in their pursuit. Salmon and steelhead runs have seen phenomenal recovery in recent years. As if that weren't enough, these waters are teeming with smallmouth bass that would be the envy of most fisheries anywhere in the country even if there were no other fish to pursue. For the avid angler it just doesn't get much better than this.

NOW FOR A SHORT DISCLAIMER

Occasionally, in an attempt to describe various equipment, tackle, and techniques, I will refer to brand names, models, or manufacturers. This is only to give you a reference point so that you will know what to look for when shopping or comparing products. This does not mean that I am endorsing these products at the exclusion of others. In most cases there are many good alternatives from which to choose. I am not on the payroll of any manufacturers, dealers, suppliers, or any other commercial concern. I do not receive any compensation from any of these people. As a general rule, when I mention any specific product it is only because that happens to be one that I am familiar with and have used with satisfactory results.

Chapter 1
THE RIVER

The Columbia River Gorge looking east up Interstate 84 from the Rowena Crest Overlook.

The mighty Columbia River drops 2,654 feet over its course from the mountains to the sea. According to the Bonneville Power Administration this river has one of the steepest descents of any U.S. waterway as it makes its 1,200-mile course to the Pacific Ocean. The force of all that falling water makes the Columbia the largest source of electrical power on the North American continent.

This giant river, with its origins in Canada, was shaped in part by events occurring some 12,000 years ago during the last great ice age. Glaciers advancing southward from arctic regions blocked the flow of the Clarks Fork and Columbia Rivers forming huge ice dams. Eventually these massive dams, holding more than 500 cubic miles of water, could no longer stand the pressure of the water, sending the entire contents of the lakes cascading down through eastern Washington.

These cataclysmic floods were repeated a number of times before the ice retreated. The volume of water released during the floods approached 18 cubic miles per hour, more than 10 times the amount of water flowing in all the rivers of the world.

The waters were estimated to be moving as fast as 60 miles per hour, emptying the lakes in a matter of two or three days. The wall of water, several hundred feet high, spilled over the normal course of the Columbia River and carved out hundreds of coulees across eastern Washington. Farther downstream the floods again followed the course of the Columbia River, producing a widening and deepening of the Columbia River Gorge.

In all, the floods traveled 550 miles and emptied into the Pacific Ocean at the mouth of the Columbia River, flooding parts of the Willamette Valley in the process.

After the ice receded, the landscape left behind came to be known as the Channeled Scablands. One of the most notable features left behind by the floods is the formation known as the Grand Coulee. This 30-mile-long canyon became the storage basin for the Columbia Basin Project launched by President Franklin Roosevelt in 1933. The Grand Coulee Dam was completed across the Columbia

THE RIVER

River in 1942, forming Lake Roosevelt, stretching 151 miles north to the Canadian Border.

Dams were also built across both ends of the Grand Coulee, forming Banks Lake. Water is pumped out of Lake Roosevelt to fill Banks Lake. This Columbia River water from Banks Lake is now used to irrigate more than 500,000 acres of the Columbia Basin. Electricity from the Grand Coulee Dam serves 11 western states.

In all, 11 hydro-power dams have now been constructed across the Columbia River in the United States and three more in Canada. Commercial barges and cruise ships ply its waters from Astoria to the Tri-Cities. Commercial traffic branches off into the Snake River at the Tri-Cities and makes it way up the Snake to Lewiston, Idaho.

The epic journey of the Lewis and Clark Corps of Discovery includes their float down the Snake and Columbia in the fall of 1805 to arrive at the Pacific Ocean in November of that year. Upon their return to mid-America in 1806 word began to spread about this majestic river and the huge potential for trade and commerce that it promised. In the 1840s the river became an important alternative mode of travel for the pioneers making their way over the Oregon Trail to the Pacific Northwest. The rest is history.

For the last 310 miles of its course to the Pacific Ocean, starting at a point about 18 miles upstream from McNary Dam, the Columbia River forms the boundary between the states of Washington and Oregon. Anglers with a license from either state can fish the

The Grand Coulee Dam, nearly a mile across and twice as high as Niagara Falls, is the largest producer of electricity in the USA and the third in the world.

entire mainstem of the river along this boundary from a boat. If you fish from the bank or back into one of the sloughs you must have a license from the state you are in. Check the fishing regulations to see where the boundaries change from Columbia River rules to tributary rules.

These anglers are hoping to hook one of the giant sturgeon that inhabit the fast tailrace directly below the dam.

McNary Dam and Lock, situated at river mile 292 is the fourth in the series starting from the mouth of the river.

The paddlewheel cruise ship Queen of the West *takes on passengers at Astoria for a trip up the Columbia and Snake rivers to Lewiston, Idaho.*

Chapter 2
GETTING AROUND ON THE RIVER

Barge hauling a decommissioned reactor from a nuclear submarine passes Irrigon on its way upstream to the Hanford Nuclear Reservation.

R unning your boat aground can be embarrassing, expensive, and even fatal. It can literally ruin your whole day. One of the first lines of defense to prevent that happening is to install a good-quality sonar unit. Many people call them fish finders and they do indeed find fish, but more importantly they tell you how much water is under your boat. No boat should be without one.

Valuable though they may be, sonar units have one serious shortcoming, they only tell you how much water is under your boat at a given moment. The transducer for most sonar units is mounted on the transom, so by the time you read the depth, the bow of your boat is already a boat length into unknown waters. Moreover, if you are ripping along at 40 mph in 10 feet of water, you could be in 10 inches of water before you can pull the throttle back.

When boating on the Columbia we have another line of defense available to us, courtesy of the United States Coast Guard. This is a system called the U.S. Aids to Navigation (ATON). Commercial vessels rely on a complex system of ATON to make sure they stay in the proper channels and avoid running aground. These aids are roughly akin to the various highway signs and traffic markers found on our nation's highways. These traffic signs on the Columbia are called "marks" by the Coast Guard. A rudimentary knowledge of just two of these marks can help pleasure boaters avoid running aground.

A Navy cutter like this one escorts each barge hauling a decommissioned nuclear reactor.

There are six different types of marks in the system, but only two of them, lateral marks and range marks, are discussed here. These marks are maintained by the United States Coast Guard.

Lateral marks are analogous to the white lines that mark the left and right edges of a highway. They mark the left and right edges of the navigable channel. Range marks are like the center line of a highway. They mark the center of the navigable channel. These marks are important to boaters because they allow you to travel at cruising speed with reasonable assurance that you won't suddenly run aground on an unseen sandbar or shoal.

Marks are not a substitute for prudent boating skills and seamanship. You must still maintain a sharp lookout for

Lateral mark 55 is home to a family of ospreys.

The paddlewheel cruise ship Queen of the West passes red lateral mark 64 heading upstream near Irrigon. Note that the mark is to the right of the ship.

Great blue herons often take over the nests after the ospreys have gone south for the winter.

Lateral mark 76 is a nun buoy just below the I-82 bridge at Umatilla.

floating debris, boats, personal watercraft and other obstructions in the water (the U.S. Coast Guard calls this "maintaining a proper lookout"). It is also important to bear in mind that when you are cruising in the navigable channel you are running with the big dogs, that is to say barges, cruise ships, Coast Guard buoy tenders, or even Navy escort ships accompanying the decommissioned nuclear submarine reactors bound for burial at the Hanford Nuclear Reservation. These guys can't stop on a dime and it is best to stay well out of their way.

As a general rule it is a good practice for pleasure boaters to stay out of the main channel except when traversing from one point to another. The advantage to running in the channel is that you know the water is deep enough to accommodate even the big ships so there is little chance of running aground. After arriving at your destination you can pull out of the main channel, especially if you intend to anchor.

The rule of thumb to remember when looking for lateral marks is "Red, Right, Returning". This means that you must always keep red marks and buoys on the right (starboard) side of your boat when returning from the sea. On the Columbia, whenever you are heading upstream you are returning from the sea.

Conversely, you must keep the green marks and buoys on the left (port) side of your boat when heading up the river.

Lateral marks take several forms. Red marks are generally triangular in shape and carry even numbers. Green marks are generally square in shape and carry odd numbers. The numbers increase as you head upstream, but they are not mile markers. Marks may be found on the bank, on pilings in the water, on larger pilings called "dolphins", or on floating buoys.

Red buoys are called nun buoys and have a conical-shaped top with the point cut off. Green buoys are called cans and are shaped as the name would imply.

Whether they appear on the bank, on pilings or dolphins, or as floating buoys, these lateral marks designate the edges of the navigable channel. The marks do not appear in pairs unless necessary, thus it is important that you remember the "Red, Right, Returning" rule. Most often you will see only one mark, either red or green. One place you can see both marks side by side is under the Interstate 82 bridge where two pairs of red and green buoys are closely spaced. Here you can see clearly that the channel under the bridge is between the red and green buoys. Downstream a short distance below Plymouth Park you

Lateral mark 75, a can buoy, is a popular spot with anglers looking for walleye or steelhead. Note the Interstate 82 Bridge and McNary Dam in the background.

Range marks near lateral mark 67 on the Washington shore near Irrigon. Note that in this photo the boat is positioned left of the channel center.

Now the vertical stripes are lined up indicating that the boat is in the center of the navigable channel.

will see green Mark 73 on the bank on the Washington shore. Farther downstream a short distance you will see red Mark 72 on a dolphin near the Oregon shore. Mark 70 is only a short distance downstream from there and it appears as a red nun buoy near the center of the river.

Range marks appear as pairs of red vertical rectangles with white or black vertical stripes. The rear mark is elevated higher than the forward mark. When you see the vertical stripes aligned with each other, your boat is in the center of the navigable channel. The marks help you stay in the center of the channel, but they won't tell you how far to stay on that course before you turn. Obviously you must turn before your boat hits the bank where the marks are situated. After your turn you can start looking for the next set of range marks to again help you stay in the center of the channel.

If you are heading upstream from under the Interstate 82 Bridge you will see a pair of range marks on the Washington shore just to the left of the lock entrance at McNary Dam. Farther downstream near Irrigon you will see a pair of range marks when heading upstream near Mark 67 on the Washington shore. These are just examples. Range marks are placed so as to guide both upstream and downstream traffic.

When your boat strays outside the boundaries defined by the lateral marks you are on your own again. Then it's just you and your sonar, so be careful until you learn which waters are safe.

For those of us who are anglers first and boaters second the lateral marks serve another useful purpose. They are excellent landmarks to help keep track of your favorite fishing holes. Perhaps coincidentally, the marks built on dolphins or pilings out in the river are good indicators of breaklines. They are usually placed in relatively shallow water, 10 or 12 feet deep located adjacent to deep water on one side (the navigable channel) and shallower water on the other side. Sometimes they are placed on underwater humps with deeper water on both sides of the shallow hump. Either way, these breaklines are excellent structure for locating walleye, smallmouth bass, and sturgeon. The marks enable you to find your way right back to the exact spot without benefit of a GPS.

Since the marks are numbered they also help us to communicate with other anglers about where to find a particular spot. Telling someone that the honey hole is located midway between Mark 57 and Mark 59 on the Washington side is easier and perhaps more precise than describing the third big bush past the tall tree.

This chapter is just a brief overview of selected ATON. If you spend much time on the river it is highly recommended that you take the Boating Skills and Seamanship course offered by the United States Coast Guard Auxiliary. It is nominally priced and covers ATON and much more valuable information about safe boating. Look in your phone book for the closest flotilla of the Coast Guard Auxiliary. Flotilla 85 is located in the Tri-Cities. Other sources of information are the Coast Guard Auxiliary Boating Safety Hotline at 1-800-368-5647 and their web site at: www.cgaux.org/index.htm. Satisfactory completion of this course satisfies the training requirement to receive the Oregon State Marine Board Boater Education Card.

The Boat Owners Association of the United States offers a free online boating basics course if you have access to the Internet. Visit their web site at: www.boatus.com

The National Ocean Service prepares river navigation charts showing the location of all these lateral marks. The charts also illustrate in topographic form what the bottom of the river looks like. Water depths are depicted by contour lines.

These charts are compiled and published by commercial concerns. One such book is called *Evergreen Pacific River Cruising Atlas: Columbia, Snake, and Willamette*, published by Evergreen Pacific Publishing Ltd., and sells locally in Hermiston. Visit their web site at: www.evergreen-pacific.com. Excerpts from this book are reproduced here with permission of the publisher. (See Chapter 10).

A Word of Caution

It is my belief, and I think statistics will back me up, that the single most important thing you can do to enhance your chances for survival on the water is to wear a personal floatation device (PFD), also called a life preserver, life jacket, or life vest. In almost every case of drowning that I read about in the newspapers it is reported that the victim was not wearing a PFD. In Oregon, it is mandatory to have a PFD in the boat for every passenger as well as one throwable PFD. Persons 12 years of age or under are required to actually wear the PFD while in the boat, whereas it is discretionary for adults.

Sometimes adults are remiss in wearing the PFD because it is too hot, too bulky, too uncomfortable or somewhat less than macho. I have found that the inflatable PFD can actually be worn all the time in all weather with a reasonable degree of comfort. If you don't like wearing one of the standard PFD styles, try wearing an inflatable. Coast Guard-approved inflatable PFDs are now readily available. They cost a little more, but in my opinion they are worth the price. Note however, that if you use one of these it is not sufficient to just keep it handy in the boat as you might do with other PFDs. You must actually be wearing it to satisfy authorities who conduct random inspections.

It should go without saying that driving a boat under the influence of intoxicants is no more prudent than driving impaired on the highway.

The author wearing a typical inflatable personal flotation device.

Chapter 3
ANCHORS AWEIGH

A cubic foot of water contains about eight gallons and weighs about 60 pounds. If you put 185,200 cubic feet of water in motion every second you have the Columbia River flowing past McNary Dam on an average day. In short, moving water is a force to be reckoned with. When you anchor your boat you come face to face with that force. Anchoring a boat on the Columbia River or any other fast-moving body of water is not a casual exercise. With that thought in mind let's take a look at a few tips that can make the experience safer. Sturgeon fishing in particular demands a thorough working knowledge of safe anchoring techniques.

The U. S. Coast Guard uses the term "Ground Tackle" to refer to the various articles of equipment needed to anchor a boat. In general, this includes the following items: line, chain, anchor, anchor puller, float, and clevises.

Start with plenty of line. Nylon is generally considered to be an excellent material for anchor line. The U. S. Coast Guard recommends that you carry a length of line equal to seven times the depth of water in which you intend to anchor. The more nearly horizontal the line, the better the anchor's holding power.

Match the anchor to your boat. When in doubt, consult your local marine dealer to get advice on the best anchor for your boat. Attach a length of chain four to six feet in length to the anchor. This will help to pull it over for a good bite and also protect the line from chafing on the bottom. Special stainless-steel clevises are available to connect the chain to the anchor and line.

Attach the line to the bow only and not to any other part of the boat. This allows the bow to face into the current. Attaching the line to the gunwale or stern can cause the boat

| *Typical ground tackle.*

to dig into the water and swamp. With the bow facing into the current, the risk of entangling the line around the motor is reduced.

Lower the anchor gently over the bow. Avoid throwing it. You don't want to discover while the anchor is in midair that the line is wrapped around your ankle.

If you expect to anchor frequently or anywhere near the tailrace of a dam, invest in an anchor puller. This is an ingenious device consisting of a floating ball and a locking device that allows the anchor line to pass through in only one direction until you manually release it. It provides several important benefits. Usually bright orange, green, or white in color, the floating ball puts other boaters on notice that you are at anchor.

| *This locking device allows the line to pass through in only one direction until you manually release it.*

The ball, positioned 25 feet or so ahead of the boat, gives you some advance warning of changes in water level or speed. It will also help to buffer the downward pull of the anchor line on the bow if the water level suddenly rises.

The puller is a labor saver. It allows you to use the power of the boat to pull the anchor up to the surface where it remains suspended directly below the ball while you simply retrieve the line without having to lift the weight of the anchor. Retrieve the anchor by driving the boat around the float and heading upstream against the current until the anchor pops to the top and hangs directly under the float. Attach the anchor line to the bow with a good sturdy quick-disconnect link. This will let you respond quickly to an emergency. If you discover, for example, that you have anchored in the path of a barge, you can disconnect and come back later when the emergency has passed. On a less urgent note, you can also disconnect to go play a big salmon or sturgeon or make a quick trip to the dock and then come back to reattach the boat to the anchor.

Keep a sharp knife handy in case you have to resort to cutting the line. This could be necessary in the event of a severe entanglement. The motor is an ever-present source of potential entanglement. A log or other large piece of floating debris could also raise this problem.

Eileen Theisen of Irrigon illustrates how easy it is to retrieve the anchor after the boat has pulled it up under the ball.

A quick disconnect is handy to permit easy separation of the anchor line from the boat.

Chapter 4

SMALLMOUTH BASS

Warm afternoon sunlight illustrates why smallmouth bass are sometimes called bronzebacks.

THE QUARRY

On October 19, 1805, when Captains Merriweather Lewis and William Clark with their Corps of Discovery camped on an island in the Columbia River at the site now called Irrigon, they did not see smallmouth bass leaping in the waters. At that time the river was inhabited by native species, including salmon, steelhead, whitefish, and sturgeon.

As immigrants pushed ever westward, especially after completion of the transcontinental railroads, many of them thought it would be a good idea if they could fish for species familiar in their former surroundings in the East, South, and Midwest, as well as their former homelands in Europe or Asia.

As a result, there was a widespread introduction of fish from other regions into the Northwest. With the aid of the railroad, many species were imported under the auspices of the Unites States Fish Commission.

According to the Washington Department of Fish and Wildlife, citing material obtained from the book *Coming of the Pond Fishes*, 1946, no longer in print, written by Ben Hur Lampman, the first exotic species were introduced into the Northwest in 1880. That is when carp were brought in and reared in a pond in Troutdale, Oregon. In 1881, several thousand of these fish escaped into the Columbia River. Now they number in the millions and are regarded as throwaway trash fish by most local anglers.

Smallmouth Bass, *Micropterous dolomieui*, were planted in the Yakima River in 1925 and again in 1934. In 1929, a six-pound smallmouth bass from the Yakima River won second place in a *Field & Stream* national contest.

Over the years smallmouth have spread to most waters throughout the Northwest including the Columbia River. They are prolific breeders and grow to respectable size here, often topping three pounds and more rarely exceeding five pounds. They are much sought after by casual and serious anglers alike.

The smallmouth bass actually has a mouth that is quite large when compared to many other species of fish. The smallmouth moniker applies, however, when this fish is compared to its cousin the largemouth bass, *Micropterous salmoides*. That fish, sometimes called "bucketmouth" for good reason, has a mouth that is truly huge.

Smallmouth are sometimes also called bronzebacks, redeyes, or brown bass. If you catch one of these fish in the late afternoon and hold it up in that warm sunlight the term bronzeback seems especially appropriate. These fish gleam with an almost metallic shiny appearance, truly a beautiful sight to behold. Smallmouth bass are members of the sunfish family which includes such popular fish as largemouth bass, crappie, and bluegill. They feed on smaller fish, crayfish, aquatic insects and occasionally even a freshwater clam.

Smallmouth hang around rocky shoreline, especially in the spring of the year. A good place to search for is a rocky point with some current flowing over a shallow ledge leading out into deeper water.

Boat anglers traditionally have the edge when it comes to fishing for walleye and many other species, but the propensity of smallmouth to frequent shorelines levels the playing field for bank anglers.

At times, the bank angler may even enjoy an advantage, working over a spot, rock by rock, with greater precision than a boater who has to be concerned with boat control as well as casting accuracy. Donning a pair of hip waders works well to extend the range of the bank angler. Either way you do it, the action can be fast and furious if you luck into a hot spot.

Smallies are aggressive feeders and fierce fighters. When hooked, they will go airborne and turn your lure every which way but loose, and they'll do that too given half a chance.

Janet Lowe of Kennewick, Washington, and a gleaming bronzeback.

They can put up a fight all out of proportion to their size. If you hook one while standing in a boat you may find yourself spinning as it circles under and around the boat.

Once brought to the net, smallmouth are second perhaps only to walleye as table fare. Many anglers practice catch and release for the large spawners, but the fish are numerous enough that you can keep some of the medium-size fish for the table without feeling guilty about depleting the species.

TACTICS

Reams and volumes are written every month about bass-fishing tactics in such publications as *Bassmaster* and *In-Fisherman* magazines. I won't attempt to plow that same ground. Here are just a few words about proven tactics that I know work well here on the mid-Columbia

Four popular lures for smallmouth are spinners, crankbaits, blades, and jigs. During summer and fall, many of the fish move out into deeper water where trolling plugs becomes a popular option. They can be found in the same waters with walleye and caught with the same lures, either plugs trolled upstream or worm harnesses baited with nightcrawlers and pulled downstream behind bottom walkers.

In the spring of the year, I like to fish for bass with small quarter-ounce in-line spinners that I make myself. Several years ago I acquired the tools needed to bend and twist the stainless steel wire used in spinners. The blades, beads, and bodies are all available from tackle catalogs like Cabela's or Bass Pro Shops. Most spinners fall into one of two types, in-line or French style. The in-line spinners are so called because the blade spins directly on the stainless wire without use of a clevis. Popular in-line commercial spinners are the Panther Martin and Vibrax. The other style uses a blade secured to the stainless wire with a clevis. Popular models of this type are the Mepps.

I like the in-line style of spinner because they seem to spin easier with less forward motion in the water. This is purely an individual bias as either style will catch lots of bass in the spring of the year.

Prior to the spawn, starting about March I take my boat back into either McCormack Slough or Paterson Slough and work close to rocky shores in shallow water. Using light spinning gear with 6-pound line cast a spinner around submerged rocks starting right at the shore and working outward. Many times the smallmouth will be in a foot of

SMALLMOUTH BASS

Casting crankbaits like Rapalas and Wiggle Warts works well in these same areas, as does casting small jigs with plastic grubs.

Much of the year I consider bass to be a by-catch from my efforts to catch walleye. In the spring this means pulling spinner/worm harnesses or jigging with jigs or blades. Starting about July my favored tactic is to pull plugs. Read about these tactics in the walleye chapter. This touches on one of the great unsung benefits of fishing the Mid-Columbia. At several times of the year, especially the fall, it is quite easy to fish for four prime freshwater species, salmon, steelhead, walleye, and smallmouth bass all at the same time in the same place, using the same lures and the same tactics. Am I smiling or what?

TROLLING (See Chapter 8)

WHERE TO GO

Starting at McNary Dam and working downstream, here are some good places to find smallmouth bass: (Refer to Charts in Chapter 10)

MCNARY LOCKS – On the Washington side, starting right at the opening of the locks, there is a rocky bank leading down to the I-82 Bridge.

MOUTH OF UMATILLA RIVER – Just upstream from the Hwy. 730 Bridge there is a wide spot in the Umatilla River that holds good numbers of smallies. Be sure to check the fishing regulations because the rules change from mainstem Columbia rules to Umatilla River rules as soon as you pass under the bridge. This is also a good spot to try for salmon or steelhead in season.

PLYMOUTH PARK – There is a nice Corps of Engineers campground and RV park directly below the I-82 Bridge on the Washington side of the river. Part of the park is situated on an island accessible from the mainland by a causeway. Smallmouth can be found all around the island, both in the causeway channel and around the river side and boat ramp as well.

LATERAL MARK 67 – On the Washington side there is a railroad riprap running along the shore upstream and downstream from lateral Mark 67 located against the shore. Trolling along this riprap is effective for smallmouth. Most of the fish are small, but you can generally find bass here much of the season from spring through fall.

PATERSON SLOUGH – A good spring fishery. Getting into the slough is a tricky business as there is an old road bed that traverses the opening to the slough. In many places this old road is less than a foot below the surface. Approach carefully. There is an opening with slightly deeper water about 2/3 of the way down from the visible part of the road bed and the Washington shore downstream from there. Once

Quarter-ounce in-line spinners can be deadly on smallmouth bass.

water or less and right up against the bank. This tactic works on up through the spawn and beyond. This tactic also works throughout the river, but starting in the sloughs gets you off to an earlier start because the water warms faster there. Generally about July I turn my attention to other tactics for bass.

Ideal cover for shoreline bass would be a rocky point with some current flowing around it. Even better if the point has a shallow ledge that leads rapidly down into deeper water.

The Highway 730 Bridge in Umatilla marks the boundary between Columbia River regulations and Umatilla River regulations.

numbers of smallmouth in the spring. Some shore fishing is done here but the boater has a definite advantage and can cover a lot more water, since the islands are not accessible from the shore.

BREAKLINES IN GENERAL – As you might expect, bass are not confined to the areas described above. They can be found throughout this section of the river in large numbers. During the summer and fall ,many of the fish move out from shore and can be found along the breaklines between lateral marks. You can pick almost any pair of lateral marks, for example between Mark 53 and Mark 55. Pull a plug upstream along that breakline in 18-25 feet of water and you are likely to hit bass.

in the slough you still have to maintain your vigilance because there are many shallow shoals interspersed with deeper waters to 20 feet or so. Check your regulations, as a Washington license is needed once you enter the slough.

BLALOCK ISLANDS – The first island below Paterson Slough is called Big Blalock 1 (refer to charts in Chapter 10) the upper end and south shore (the shore facing Oregon) are good places to find bass as are the islands directly downstream from Blalock. Below Big Blalock 1 are numerous dangerous shoals all the way from there to Boardman. If you venture out of the navigable channel, exercise extreme caution.

MCCORMACK SLOUGH – Another good springtime haunt. Enter from the downstream end of Long Walk Island and proceed with caution.

CROW BUTTE PARK – There is a pumphouse and a series of small islands and rocky outcrops along the Washington shore across from the boat ramp at the park. This is a good place in the spring if you get in there before the whole area becomes choked with milfoil.

THREE MILE CANYON – Across the river from the Oregon boat ramp at Three Mile Canyon near lateral Mark 27 on the Washington side, there is a series of small islands that hold good

The railroad riprap along lateral Mark 67 on the Washington shore upstream from Irrigon is a good place to try for bass.

Chapter 5

WALLEYE

You can grab a bass by the lips, but you don't want to try that with a walleye.

THE QUARRY

These toothy critters called walleye that now occupy our Columbia River waters are viewed with mixed feelings by both anglers and fish management authorities alike. Known in scientific circles as *Stizostedion vitreum*, their exact origin in local waters is somewhat murky, but according to the Washington Department of Fish and Wildlife (WDFW). walleye were first verified in Banks Lake in 1962. Shortly afterward they showed up in Franklin Roosevelt Lake which is connected to Banks Lake by huge pipes and pumps. From there they have spread throughout the Columbia mainstem from Canada to nearly the Pacific Ocean.

How the walleye got into Banks Lake is uncertain. but WDFW reports there are two theories: they were released into Lake Roosevelt by the U.S. Fish and Wildlife Service in the 1950s using fry from Lake Oneida in New York. or. they were planted into Devil's Lake in the 1930s and were absorbed into Banks Lake when Devil's Lake was inundated by the Columbia Basis Irrigation Project.

However they managed to get here or whatever your opinion of them. for better or worse. it looks like walleye are here to stay. In the vernacular of today's youth. we might just as well "get used to it".

In spite of their dubious or perhaps even nefarious origins. walleye have become an important factor on the overall sport fishing scene in both Washington and Oregon. Long one of the most popular sport fish in northern and central states including Michigan. Wisconsin. Minnesota.

Eileen Theisen of Irrigon holds a large northern pikeminnow.

however, they are not the primary predator on salmonids in the Columbia. That distinction belongs to the northern pikeminnow. According to WDFW, pikeminnow, formerly called squawfish, even without the deadly teeth, consume almost four times as many salmon and steelhead smolts as walleye, smallmouth bass, and channel catfish combined. The Oregon Department of Fish and Wildlife (ODFW) has studied ways to control walleye as part of an effort to reduce predation on salmonids. One apparently obvious way to do this would be to liberalize creel limits. Presumably, if anglers catch and keep more walleye it would leave fewer in the river to eat little salmon. Unfortunately for the salmon it doesn't work out that way.

Studies documented by ODFW show that it is primarily little walleye, those less than 12 inches in length, that favor salmon smolts in their diets. Larger walleye turn their attention to sculpins and other prey like suckers and pikeminnow as they grow larger. Thus, liberalizing creel limits may have little if any effect on salmon predation. In the John Day pool it is unlikely that anglers will catch a walleye smaller than 12 inches, and should it happen, it is even more unlikely that the angler would keep the fish.

Starting in the year 2000 both states liberalized the walleye creel limit on the mid-Columbia from five fish to 10

Illinois, North and South Dakota, these relative newcomers to the Pacific Northwest have attracted a large and dedicated following.

Not prized for their fighting ability, walleye have other redeeming qualities, not the least of which is that they grow big. Nowhere is that more true than right here on the John Day pool of the Columbia, also known as Lake Umatilla. Each year sees several reported in the 16 pound class. On March 3, 2002, Kimo Gabriel of Hermiston, Oregon, caught and released a walleye weighing in at 18.90 pounds on a certified scale. By happenstance Gabriel was able to claim a new Washington State walleye record even though he released the fish. Rod McKenzie and Lara Arriola of High Desert Marine in Hermiston brought their certified scale to the Irrigon Marina to get the weight. Luckily, an Oregon State Police Fish and Wildlife Officer was at hand who could certify that the fish was indeed a walleye. Ordinarily an angler would need to bring the fish into a Washington Fish and Wildlife office for positive identification of the species. Gabriel's fish eclipsed the previous Washington record of 18.76 pounds. He got his lunker on a jig and plastic worm. The Oregon state record as of this writing is 19 pounds, 15.3 ounces.

The other redeeming quality of walleye is that they make excellent table fare. The flesh cooks up firm, white, and flaky with very little "fishy" taste, reminiscent of fresh halibut. They can be prepared any way you like to cook fish.

Walleye are viewed with some trepidation by fish and wildlife managers and some anglers because they are a known predator on other fish, most notably native salmon and steelhead. In spite of their ferocious toothy appearance,

This northern pikeminnow is the most notorious predator on salmon and steelhead smolts to be found in the Columbia River.

fish. The minimum size requirement was also lifted. opening the door for anglers to keep up to 10 fish under 18 inches whereas previously none were allowed. There are still some constraints on the maximum sizes that can be kept.

The practical effect of this new rule remains to be seen. at least on the John Day pool. This pool is noted for big fish. Not many fish under 18 inches are generally caught. although the 2003 season produced larger numbers of undersize fish than seen for many previous years. The other practical consideration is that limits of fish are rare. even under the previous five fish limit. Even skilled anglers find it difficult to catch more than five walleye of any size on a given outing.

The best proof of this is to attend a few of the weigh-ins for local walleye tournaments. The money is usually won by a few big fish rather than limits of smaller fish.

Walleye are members of the perch family. Locally the only other member of this family is the yellow perch. They are also among the group of fish called "warmwater" fish including bass. bluegills. crappies. and catfish. This group is also known as "spiney rays" because of their sharp fins. This distinguishes them from the "coldwater" fish that include salmon. steelhead, trout, char, and whitefish.

THE TACTICS

Three popular tactics for catching walleye include pulling plugs. pulling spinners with bottom walkers, and jigging with either jigs or blade baits. Spinners and jigs are generally sweetened with part or all of a nightcrawler. Plugs and blade baits are fished without any added bait.

Slow presentations using jigs or blades are favored during the cold months of winter and early spring. Worm harnesses behind bottom walkers are popular in spring and summer and pulling plugs is popular in summer and fall. These are just generalizations and not hard, fast rules. The chapter on trolling describes the tactics of pulling plugs for walleye and other species.

BOTTOM WALKING WITH SPINNERS

Bottom walking is a medium-speed presentation that works well in spring and summer and is actually suitable any time of year. It works as the name implies. Start with a special type of sinker called a bottom walker. It is a stiff piece of wire about a foot long with a lead weight cast onto it about two-thirds of the way up. In use, the tip of the wire scratches along the bottom. The leader and spinner harness are attached to a shorter length of wire forming a Y at the top of the bottom walker. keeping them a few inches off the bottom to reduce snags.

Start with a bottom walker with a weight of about 2 or 2.5 ounces. That works well on most places on the river. Attach the spinner/worm harness with a leader about 3 or 4 feet long. This will have two hooks snelled on it with a spinner blade. a few colored beads. and a floater of some kind to help keep the worm off the bottom. If you snell your

Spinner/worm harnesses are generally fished with a live nightcrawler, part of which can be seen here in this walleye's mouth.

| *Typical bottom walker sinkers.*

| *Typical spinner/worm harnesses.*

own leaders use 10 or 12 pound test low visibility line rated for abrasion resistance. Ultra low-visibility Trilene XT works well with #2 or #4 octopus style hooks.

Spinner blades come in a wide variety of colors. Gold, silver, chartreuse and bright orange are all good choices. If you make your own spinner harnesses you can get quick change clevises that enable you to change blades as you fish. Place the upper hook directly into the nose of the nightcrawler and the lower hook about half way down the night crawler so that the worm stretches out straight as it trails through the water.

Hook the main line onto the top of the bottom walker using a Duo-Lock snap and you are ready to start fishing. Drop the bottom walker over the side of the boat. Put just enough forward speed on the boat to get the spinner blade spinning and make sure the leader is trailing out straight without any tangles. Most walleye anglers troll downstream.

WALLEYE

Spinner harnesses can be deadly when a slow to medium presentation is called for.

Northland Whistler Jigs, shown here with added trailer hooks. These are often sweetened with live nightcrawler or some kind of soft plastic grub or curly tail.

Drop the bottom walker until it hits bottom and then adjust carefully from there. Let out just enough line so that the tip of the wire is barely ticking along the bottom. If you let out too much line the bottom walker can lay over and become much more prone to snagging up. As the depth of the water varies, take in and let out line as necessary to keep the tip of the wire ticking along the bottom at frequent intervals. Generally, the electric motor will work best for this technique as you are moving very slowly. Adjust the weight and speed so that the line trails out into the water at about a 45-degree angle.

If you use one of the non-stretch superlines as the main line you will have much more sensitivity than with monofilament and you will be able to feel the wire ticking on the bottom much more readily. If you don't know what depth the fish are in, somewhere in the 15-30-foot range would be a good depth to start. In the dead of winter or cold of early spring even deeper into the 40-plus-foot range would be worth a try.

Jigs

There are literally dozens of styles, colors, sizes, and weights of jig. Since the walleye are generally found in deep water during winter and early spring you will need a fairly heavy jig, half to three-quarters of an ounce, to find bottom. Northland Whistler Jigs are popular here as are plain lead head jigs. Many anglers sweeten the jigs with half a nightcrawler or a piece of soft plastic such as a grub or twin tail twister. Some use both nightcrawler and soft plastic. Chartreuse and white are popular colors. If you use a large piece of nightcrawler you may want to add a stinger hook to avoid short bites.

Once the jig is rigged to your satisfaction it is just a matter of dropping it over the side until if finds bottom. Let it bump gently along the bottom as the boat drifts downstream. Most anglers try to keep the line nearly vertical, which may call for some correction with the trolling motor, especially if there is any wind.

BLADES

Blades are a specialized form of jig. They are fished in a similar manner, but without any soft plastic or nightcrawler added. Because there are two exposed treble hooks on most blades you can't allow them to drag bottom as you would with a jig that remains upright. Instead, drop the blade to the bottom, but don't leave it there. As soon as it touches bottom, twitch it back up a foot or so. Continue doing this as you drift downstream.

With each twitch of the rod tip you can feel a pronounced vibration from the blade. This is evidently the feature that makes blades so deadly. One advantage to blades is that you can immediately feel when the blade has become fouled by a piece of debris or has tangled on the line. When this happens just bring it up and clear it. Blades are not much to look at, with many being a plain silver or brass in color. Others are painted, but in spite of their plain appearance they catch a lot of walleye and other species as well. My neighbor, Steve Daulton, brought up a 10-foot sturgeon with one recently. Of course, the contest didn't last long after that monster went airborne and got a look at our boat. This is where the sharp knife came in handy.

TROLLING (See Chapter 8)

WHERE TO GO

Whereas bass are often found close to shore, walleye are more likely to be farther out in the mainstem of the river. The walleye fishery is primarily a boat fishery and here the bank angler is at a definite disadvantage.

Starting at McNary Dam and working downstream, here are some good places to find walleye: (Refer to charts in Chapter 10).

McNARY LOCKS – Draw a line from the opening of the lock at McNary Dam down to the rocky point directly upstream from the I-82 Bridge. The upper half of this region, including the deep channel that parallels the Washington shore below the lock is a good place to find walleye in summer and fall. Watch the sonar close because there are some rocky underwater humps here that can damage your boat if you are not careful.

Steve Daulton of Irrigon nailed this nice seven-pound walleye on a white blade bait.

THE GREEN CAN – Directly below the I-82 bridge is lateral Mark 75, a green can buoy out near the middle of the river, locally referred to as the "green can" for obvious reasons. The entire area from the green can to the Washington shore above Plymouth Park is a popular walleye hole in summer and fall. Starting in late fall this is also a popular spot among those who like to fish walleye at night. A bonus feature of this spot is that it also yields an occasional salmon or steelhead for anglers after walleye.

PLYMOUTH PARK – The Washington shore starting directly below the island at Plymouth Park is a good spring fishery. Some anglers work fairly close to shore in ten feet of water or less, but you can pick your depth by working farther out toward the middle of the river.

MOUTH OF THE UMATILLA RIVER – This is a good summer and fall fishery. In this instance you don't go up the Umatilla River, but stay out in the Columbia mainstem outside the mouth. Various depths are available starting from shallow near shore to 25 feet or more out toward the middle of the Columbia. Also a good spot for salmon or steelhead in season.

WALLEYE

LATERAL MARK 72 – Downstream a short distance from the mouth of the Umatilla River is lateral Mark 72 on a pylon out in the river near the Oregon shore. You can work this area starting from lateral Mark 70. a red nun buoy downstream from Mark 72 all the way up to the mouth of the Umatilla River. Most anglers favor the Oregon side here. But the Washington side yields fish as well.

THE COUNTY LINE – So called because this is the approximate location of the Umatilla-Morrow County line

This 2.5-pound smallmouth succumbed to a white blade bait.

Lateral Mark 62 is the first mark you encounter as you head upstream from the Irrigon Marina.

(Oregon) as marked by a sign on Hwy. 730. Generally it includes the entire area from lateral mark 70 on the upstream end to lateral mark 64 downstream. Most anglers work the Oregon side ranging from close to shore out to the middle of the river where it meets the navigable channel.

LATERAL MARK 62-64 BREAKLINE – Just outside the Irrigon Marina. as you head upstream. you will encounter lateral mark 62 first and then lateral mark 64. Draw a line between these two marks and you will locate a sharp breakline that drops from about one foot deep to about 50 feet deep. This is a popular spring fishery starting as early as February and continuing right up through the spawn in April or May.

CAUTION: Make sure you stay to the Washington (north) side of these marks. This is a spot where familiarity with the "Red, Right, Returning" rule can save you a lot of grief. Driving a boat inside these marks toward the Oregon shore can cost you a lower unit or worse. The water here rises rapidly to a foot or so in depth. At times when the river is low you can even see a few rocks protruding above the surface. When you exit the marina at Irrigon don't make a sharp right to head upstream or you will proceed right up onto this shoal. Head out toward the middle of the river until you are well clear of mark 62 before heading upstream.

MARK 59 – The first lateral mark you encounter when heading downstream from the Irrigon marina is lateral Mark 59. This mark sits up on an underwater hump with deeper water on both sides, with the deepest water to the Oregon side where the navigable channel runs. Pulling plugs or spinners on the breaklines on both sides of this mark is a popular summer and fall walleye hotspot.

PATERSON DRIFT – Proceeding farther downstream to the Irrigon fish hatchery brings you to another favored walleye haunt. This is a good drift starting in February and extending right through the season into fall. The drift starts toward the Washington side opposite the hatchery and extends all the way down to the mouth of the Paterson Slough. During the pre-spawn you will want to use a slow presentation with jigs or blades and work deeper water starting around 40 feet or so. Later, as the season progresses, you can switch to spinners and plugs and work closer toward the Washington shore in shallower water running 18-25 feet or shallower.

LATERAL MARK 51 – Just below the Paterson drift you will come to lateral Mark 51 near Blalock Island. This is another all-season walleye haunt. Be prepared to lose some tackle here because this drift is notoriously snaggy, but some big fish come out of here, especially early during the pre-spawn period.

FORK IN THE ROAD – At Blalock Island you are forced to choose between two routes to proceed farther downstream. The navigable channel runs toward the Oregon side and the old North Channel proceeds down the Washington side. The safest route is to follow the navigable channel, but the old North Channel is safe enough if you proceed with caution. Just be aware that there are no lateral marks remaining in the old North Channel to keep you in safe water. Fortunately, you can find walleye by going either way.

GLADE CREEK – Down the old North Channel you will come to Glade Creek. This is a good all-season drift.

BREAKLINES IN GENERAL – As you proceed down the navigable channel from Blalock Island you will find lateral marks all along. The river widens out here as you approach Boardman. You can find walleye all along here on breaklines too numerous to list here, but extending all the way downstream to lateral mark 36 below the Boardman marina.

EYEBALL FISH LOCATOR – Walleye enthusiasts get three opportunities each year to find out first-hand where the fish are hanging out. The Columbia River Walleye Circuit sponsors three tournaments each year, the Smoker Craft Spring Walleye Classic in March, the High Desert Marine Walleye Derby in July, and the Oregon Governor's Cup in September. The first two contests are held in Boardman and the Governor's Cup is held in Umatilla.

The two-person teams who enter these tournaments represent many of the best walleye anglers from throughout the Pacific Northwest. In addition to their travel and lodging expenses each team invests at least $200 in entry fees. Many of them spend much of the week preceding the tournament pre-fishing to locate the fish and refine their tactics.

After investing all this time and money you can bet these expert anglers are going to head to spots that they feel hold the best chance to find fish. You can share in this knowledge for just the price of your time and gas. All you have to do is launch your boat at any of the marinas between Umatilla and Boardman, drive up and down the river and see where the experts are. Just remember that they are working for high stakes, so the courteous thing to do is stay out of their way. This is a big river. There is no need to crowd your fellow anglers. After the tournaments are over you can go back and work the same spots previously staked out by the experts.

If you want to avoid getting caught in a crowd of boats at weigh-in time it is a good idea to launch your boat at one of the marinas where the tournament is not being held. Later in the afternoon, usually starting about 2:30 PM you can attend the weigh-in and see the big money-winning fish brought in. You will also have a chance to win some prizes at the raffles held in conjunction with these tournaments.

Lateral Mark 64 is the second mark you encounter as you head upstream from the Irrigon Marina.

Chapter 6
WHITE STURGEON

A sturgeon with its mouth fully extended. Note the barbels.

Author Arnold Theisen with a sturgeon showing the sharp bony plates called scutes.

THE QUARRY

QUESTION: Where does an eight-foot sturgeon go when hooked from a 13-foot Boston Whaler?

ANSWER: Anywhere it wants to.

If you want to get your heart pounding just try watching an eight-foot sturgeon come crashing through the surface of the water in a desperate attempt to throw your hook.

In a scene reminiscent of the movie "Jaws", when one of these monsters suddenly looms up beside the boat, you can't help but wonder briefly just who has caught whom.

If Herman the Sturgeon could talk he would probably shrug "whatever" when asked about all the hoopla surrounding the arrival of the new millennium in the year 2000 (or 2001 if you are a mathematical purist). After all, when your ancestors have been hanging around the neighborhood for 200,000 millennia, what's one more millennium, more or less?

Eileen Theisen of Irrigon gets up close and personal with Herman the Sturgeon, the patriarch of the sturgeon pond at Bonneville Dam.

Herman the Sturgeon is the patriarch of the sturgeon pond at the Bonneville Fish Hatchery located at Bonneville Dam. This 60-plus-year-old fish is 10 feet long and weighs in at a hefty 450 pounds, about double that of his seven-foot pond mates.

Herman and others of his kind, the white sturgeon, scientific name *Acipenser transmontanus*, are the ultimate survivors. They watched those Johnnie-come-lateleys, the dinosaurs, come and go like a flash in the pan.

If you could jump into a time machine and go back to fish in the Columbia River 200 million years ago, the sturgeon you caught then would look essentially the same as the one you would catch today. These magnificent creatures, the largest anadromous fish in North America, have survived virtually unchanged over these 200 million years.

Anadromous fish normally live part of their life cycle in salt water. Construction of the dams on the Columbia and Snake Rivers has left a large population of white sturgeon landlocked. True to their survivalist nature, these fish have not let the dams deter them from continued propagation of

their species. They continue to live their entire life cycle in the freshwater pools created by the dams.

Sturgeon populations unfettered by dams range from Mexico to Alaska. Other common names for these fish are Pacific sturgeon, Oregon sturgeon, Columbia sturgeon, and Sacramento sturgeon.

White sturgeon have been known to grow to 20 feet in length and weigh more than 1,800 pounds. They can live more than 100 years.

In the Columbia and Snake River drainages sturgeon range from the Pacific Ocean at the mouth of the Columbia River all the way into Canada and on the Snake into Washington and Idaho. For the last 310 river miles the Columbia forms the boundary between Oregon and Washington. Over this course there are four large hydroelectric dams, starting with Bonneville at about mile 146 (measured from the mouth of the river).

Proceeding up the river the next dam is at The Dalles at about mile 192, then John Day at about mile 216, and finally McNary at about mile 292. This entire stretch of the river is prime sturgeon territory, especially those areas immediately below each dam and several miles downstream from each dam.

In a practical vein, there are probably not many 20- footers to be seen these days, but there are 10- and 12-footers to be found in the tailrace of each dam. The sturgeon pond at Bonneville Dam offers both above ground and underwater viewing of these monster fish.

A timeline exhibit posted at the Bonneville Dam viewing window traces the history of the Columbia River sturgeon. Some 10,000 years ago native people harvested sturgeon and other fish for sustenance. In the 1840s and 1850s, pioneers on the Oregon Trail also utilized this resource. From the 1860s to the 1890s the fishery increased in intensity, first as a bycatch of the salmon fishery and then as a targeted fishery. In 1892 the sturgeon harvest peaked at 5.5 million pounds with fish averaging seven feet and 150 pounds. By 1898 over-harvesting had severely depleted the population and both Washington and Oregon had instituted controls to prevent complete extinction.

Careful management of the resource by both states has restored the fishery to the point that controlled harvests can now be allowed for commercial anglers, Indian Tribes, and sport anglers. By 1997, the estimated population of white sturgeon below Bonneville Dam was one million with 495,000 measuring three to six feet in length.

Retention quotas are established for each of the pools on the river. The numbers of sturgeon allowed to be retained is subject to change with each season. When the quota has been reached, anglers are not allowed to keep any more sturgeon until the start of the next season. In recent years the quota on the John Day pool has not been reached except for the year 2002 which had a smaller quota than previous years. These restrictions are posted on signs at each of the

Eileen Theisen of Irrigon holds a white sturgeon that looks much like a shark except for its mouth.

marinas and can be found on the Department of Fish and Wildlife web sites for each state. When the numerical quotas have been reached. notices are posted at the marinas and publicized by other means as well. After a quota has been reached anglers are permitted to continue fishing for sturgeon. but they must release all that are caught.

Except for their mouths sturgeon present an overall shark-like appearance Instead of scales they have a rough skin with five rows of bony plates called scutes These scutes are very sharp and serve as an effective deterrent to potential predators. Under the nose are four sensory whisker-like protrusions called barbels that aid them in the search for food as they root along the bottom of the river.

The sturgeon has an unusual extendible and retractable tube-like mouth that serves like a kind of vacuum cleaner for picking up food. Their diet consists of fish, shellfish, crayfish. shrimp. and other aquatic animals. Much to the dismay of the angler. these fish are amazingly adept at nibbling the bait off a hook without hooking themselves. This propensity to nibble creates one of the more exciting aspects of this sport. When you set the hook you don't know if you are laying into a two-footer or an eight-footer with the strength to pull you right out of the boat. But you'll find out soon enough. If it's one of those eight-footers you'd better hang on for the ride of your life.

Sturgeon are an underrated game fish with remarkable fighting ability. It is not uncommon for sturgeon to head for the surface and thrash the top of the water several times in an attempt to shake the hook. They don't come quietly to the boat. They can strip the line from your reel down to the backing before you get the anchor pulled.

These primeval fish aren't beautiful like salmon or steelhead. By some standards they might even be called ugly. And sturgeon fishing can be a messy. stinky business. If you are lucky enough to pull a keeper into your boat it can slash you. your clothing and anything else nearby into shreds with those razor-sharp scutes. Cleaning a four- or five-foot keeper

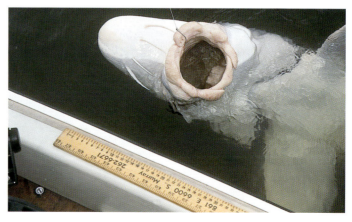

The sturgeon's mouth extends and retracts. Here it is shown mostly retracted.

isn't as simple as gutting a trout. It's more like butchering a hog. But the payoff comes in the eating when you pull the filets from the smoker. These prehistoric bottom-dwellers yield a treat like no other.

TACTICS

Sturgeon fishing is not best characterized as a sophisticated art form. Robert Redford probably won't be making a movie like "A River Runs Through It" about sturgeon fishing. The recipe here calls for stout tackle, strong line, heavy sinkers, big hooks, stinky bait, a comfortable place to sit and lots of patience.

Serious preparation is required in the tackle department. Set aside your bass and walleye gear. Even salmon and steelhead gear won't be sufficient. You need a really stout pole and a heavy-duty reel spooled with line testing at least 30 pounds and maybe more. I've caught several keepers using a Penn 209 reel with 30- pound line, but that is about as light as I would recommend. Of course, that was fishing from a boat. Off the bank you need even heavier tackle. Most people use a 12-foot pole and a saltwater style reel, either level wind or spinning.

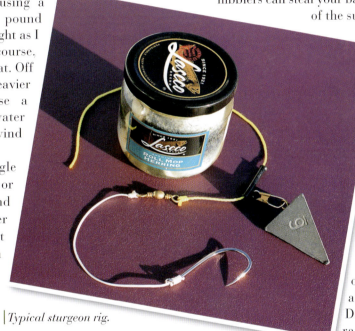

Typical sturgeon rig.

Tie up some single barbless hooks, size 6/0 or larger, on 72- or 96-pound braided nylon leader approximately two feet long. Put a sliding snap on the main line and join the main line to the leader with a large barrel swivel. Hang the sinker on the sliding snap. Weight varies with the speed of the current, but you need enough to hold the bait on the bottom. In slow or medium current six ounces is usually enough. Up near the dam you may need 14 or 16 ounces of lead. With the sliding snap, changing to different size sinkers is easy.

With the tackle ready, the next consideration is bait. There are numerous baits used to target sturgeon, including shrimp, squid, herring, and other specialty concoctions. The bait most popular and readily available in this region is roll mop herring. This pickled herring comes packed in jars and can be purchased in all the local tackle shops and grocery stores. It should be kept refrigerated.

Carry a spool of thread in your tackle box. Regular sewing thread works, but there is also a special elastic thread sold specifically for tying on sturgeon bait. Cut a chunk of

herring filet big enough to mostly hide the hook. A piece about one inch by three inches will do for starters. Put the hook through the herring a few times and then tie the herring on securely with thread. After wrapping the thread several times, tie it off with a couple of half-hitches.

With the boat anchored over a promising hole, chuck the whole business over the side of the boat and you are sturgeon fishing. Keep a tight line. Periodically check to make sure the bait is staying on the bottom and you don't have a loop in the line. You can do this by pulling back on the rod and letting the sinker drop back down. If you can't feel the sinker thump the bottom there is a chance that the current is picking it up. If that happens you need to either let out more line or add more weight or both until you are sure you can feel the sinker thump bottom each time you drop it back down.

Now comes the waiting game. Sturgeon fishing is a real exercise in suspense. Bring a good supply of bait. These nibblers can steal your bait in spite of your best efforts. Part of the suspense is knowing that the size of the nibble doesn't necessarily signal the size of the fish. On the other hand, they don't always nibble. On occasion the first time you know you have a bite is when the rod doubles over and the reel starts to sing.

Stay ready to release the anchor. If it is a really big one the best chance you have of getting it to the side of the boat for a photo is to follow it around with the boat.

Carry a ruler to check the size of the fish once you get it alongside the boat. On the John Day pool the legal keeper size ranges from 48 to 60 inches as of this writing. Farther down the river there are places where 42-inch fish may be kept. Just be sure to check the regulations for the area you fish.

Generally speaking a landing net is not all that effective for getting a keeper into the boat. If possible, I prefer to put on a pair of gloves and grab the fish by the tail on one end and the gill plate or leader on the other and just hoist it into the boat. With a five-footer this could be a two-person task. Watch out for the scutes, some of which can be razor sharp. Another trick I sometimes try is to carry a length of rope five or six feet long. Tie a loop in both ends. Thread the rope through one of the loops to form a noose. The other loop serves as a hand hold. If you can't get a good grip on the fish alongside the boat, slip the noose over the tail of the fish and cinch it up. Then if the line or leader breaks or the hook comes out you will still have a good hold on the fish.

Remember that it is now illegal to bring oversize fish out of the water. Either cut the line or get a sturdy pair of pliers and remove the hook while the fish is alongside the boat.

WHERE TO GO

If you glance to your right (east) as you travel northbound over the I-82 Bridge at Umatilla you will look down on what is probably the most popular stretch of sturgeon water on this entire stretch of the river. This is the tailrace below McNary Dam.

On any calm day you are likely to see sturgeon anglers anchored along here all the way from the bridge upstream to the deadline immediately below the dam. The deadline is marked by a sign on the entrance to the McNary Lock on the Washington side and a sign on shore on the Oregon side. This is the line beyond which you are not allowed to take a boat.

These waters are dangerous to the inexperienced or careless boater. Many boats and several of their occupants have been lost here over the years. It seems each year sees at least one accident with tragic consequences. The swift moving water makes proper anchoring techniques very critical (see Chapter 3 above). If you've not fished here before I would recommend you make your first trip with a licensed professional guide or an experienced boater who can show you the ropes on your first time out.

This area is popular for good reason. Here are to be found some of the biggest sturgeon. The tailraces below each dam hold many of the 10- and 12-footers. Your chance to hook one of these monsters is probably better here than most other places on the river. That's not to say there aren't big fish elsewhere because there certainly are.

I don't mind admitting that the swift water below the dam makes me a little uneasy. If you share that feeling with me there are still plenty of other places to find sturgeon of all sizes. In fact, it's not a good idea to get fixated on specific spots on the river because these fish tend to move around a lot. Even when you are fishing in spots that have previously held fish I recommend that if you don't get a bite in an hour or so, move to another spot. There is simply no way to predict just where these fish will be on a given day.

Having said that, I can still recommend a number of places that have proven productive over recent years.

Moving downstream from the dam, the area along the railroad riprap at lateral mark 67 on the Washington shore has been productive for both bank anglers and boaters. The water reaches 40 feet or more within casting distance from shore. Good water extends from here all along the Washington side of the navigable channel on down to the area across from the Irrigon marina. Below the marina on the Oregon side is also a good spot to try. My personal best fish, an 8-plus-footer came from this spot. I've also seen 10-footers come out of here.

The deep channel close to the Oregon shore just below the Irrigon fish hatchery sees a lot of action both from the bank and from boats. Boaters can fish both sides of this deep channel which drops to 80 feet in places, while bank anglers are limited to the Oregon shore. This hole extends from the fish hatchery down to the grain elevator, also on the Oregon shore. Avoid anchoring in the middle of this channel as that is where the navigable channel runs. The south side of Blalock Island, the side facing the Oregon shore, out in or near the navigable channel is a popular area and worth a try on any given day.

In 2001 the Washington and Oregon Departments of Fish and Wildlife conducted a sturgeon survey on the John Day pool. Using set lines they caught and tagged several thousand fish. During the course of this study they determined that this pool has a healthy and thriving population of white sturgeon.

Informal discussions with one of the members of the survey team indicated that the preponderance of the sturgeon population in the John Day pool can be found in the section of the river above Arlington. He also suggested that if you want to try some promising areas with less fishing pressure, the old North Channel between Blalock Island and

Crystal Flinn, 13, of Layton, Utah, with a 48-inch keeper.

Jack Collins of Hermiston with a 57-inch, 42-pound keeper.

Glade Creek would be a good area to explore, as well as the area just outside the bay leading into Crow Butte Park.

EYEBALL FISH LOCATOR– The spots I've mentioned here just scratch the surface. As I mentioned before, sturgeon roam all over this river in a wide range of depths. Sturgeon anglers are easy to spot. Just look for the boats sitting at anchor with a big colorful ball floating out ahead of the boat. As you travel up and down the river keep an eye out for single or groups of boats consistently working certain spots. This can give you a pretty good clue as to where the fish are to be found. Again, courtesy should prevail. The river is big enough that there is no need to crowd fellow anglers.

A tidewater barge heads upstream in the deep channel along the Irrigon Fish Hatchery and the grain elevator.

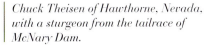

Chuck Theisen of Hawthorne, Nevada, with a sturgeon from the tailrace of McNary Dam.

Chapter 7
SALMON AND STEELHEAD

The author with a 25-pound chinook caught on a purple quarter-ounce Hot Lips called a Grape Ape.

Salmon and steelhead are lumped together in this chapter because for the most part they run together on this part of the river, the seasons largely overlap, and the tactics are often similar. That's likely not true on other parts of the river and other waters, but, unfortunately, this part of the Mid-Columbia is not best described as prime salmonid habitat. Those targeting these fish exclusively would do better farther downstream or upstream on the Hanford Reach or up the Snake River near the confluence with the Clearwater River or into Hells Canyon.

Nevertheless, those same fish pass right through here on their way upstream and they do provide ample opportunity for enterprising anglers to pursue them as they go by. This has been especially true in recent years when respectable runs have again materialized after a long dry spell.

Fishing for salmon and steelhead can be described as hours and hours of boredom punctuated by a few minutes of sheer pandemonium. To be sure, pandemonium is what you get when you hook into a big chinook or steelhead. The legendary fighting ability of these fish is no doubt one of the reasons they have acquired such a mythic aura among anglers in these parts. Add the facts that they can provide excellent table fare and that they are among the few species native to these waters for millions of years and it is no wonder that salmon and steelhead are two of the very icons that define the Pacific Northwest.

THE QUARRY

Chinook Salmon
Here in quater-ounce the Pacific Northwest the chinook salmon, *Oncorhynchus tshawytscha,* also

Steve Daulton of Irrigon got this 12-pound chinook casting a black and yellow Vibrax spinner just above the Highway 730 Bridge over the Umatilla River.

called king salmon, is both literally and figuratively the king. Northwesterners have voted with their wallets, spending hundreds of millions of dollars each year on salmon restoration efforts. These kings of the river are the largest of Pacific salmon species reaching 58 inches in length and over 100 pounds, although they are more commonly seen in lengths to three feet and weights to 30 pounds.

By the time the kings have reached this part of the river they have traveled some 300 miles since leaving the Pacific Ocean. As a result they are starting to show some wear, often turning noticeably dark and with eating quality less than prime. Many are considered to be "smokers" by local anglers. Nevertheless, they have not lost their ability to entice seasoned and novice anglers alike, many with a dedication bordering on fanaticism.

Steelhead

These sea-run rainbow trout, *Oncorhynchus mykiss*, follow the same primordial urge as the salmon as they make their way up the Columbia to the headwaters of their spawning grounds. Unlike salmon, they are not genetically programmed to die after one spawning. Perhaps for this reason they are generally in better shape when they get here. Many are still chrome bright and most still offer excellent table fare. They are capable of returning to the ocean after spawning and then coming back another season to spawn again, although relatively few actually do this.

According to an article by Bill Monroe in the *Oregonian* newspaper all steelhead runs east of The Dalles, which would include all fish on this portion of the river, are summer steelhead. They are reputed to have higher fat reserves because of their longer journey inland. Numberswise, the larger runs are the winter runs returning to coastal streams and the lower Columbia.

TACTICS

Trolling with plugs is the most popular tactic employed by salmon and steelhead anglers on this part of the river. Those tactics are described in the chapter on trolling (Chapter 8).

For salmon, another technique often used with good results is to anchor the boat in a promising spot with a reasonable amount of current and let the current work a big Flatfish or Kwikfish (size K14 or K16, for example) out behind the boat. These lures produce good action in slow moving water. For added attraction try tying a small filet of herring onto the belly of the lure. Let the lure out behind the boat 50 feet or so, put the rod in a holder and sit back. Salmon will hit this offering without any added action imparted by the angler.

Many anglers prefer to go after steelhead with natural baits. Shrimp, either dyed red or natural color, and salmon or steelhead roe are popular baits used by boaters and bank anglers alike. These are generally fished below a slip bobber and left to drift with the wind and current.

WHERE TO GO

Areas directly above and below McNary Dam are the most popular spots for salmon and steelhead. This is a seasonal fishery, with fall generally producing the best fishing. The season usually starts around August first, but the best fishing starts about October and continues on into December. A limited spring run season also has been opened for chinook in recent years.

Below the I-82 Bridge, lateral mark 75, commonly called the green can, is a good place to troll for steelhead. Here you might want to try backtrolling as well. Likewise, just downstream from the Umatilla Marina and RV Park is where the Umatilla River empties into the Columbia. Pulling plugs in the mainstem of the Columbia River just opposite the mouth of the Umatilla River is a good place to find salmon and steelhead both. This also is a good place to try anchoring with Flatfish or Kwikfish as described in the preceding paragraph.

Other tactics can be employed in the mouth of the Umatilla River. Some success can be had by anchoring right in the mouth where it meets the Columbia and casting with spinners or crankbaits. Rainbow-colored Vibrax

Blue Fox spinners and crankbaits such as Wiggle Warts can be productive. You can continue this tactic right on into the Umatilla River and up past the Highway 730 bridge, but make sure you check the regulations. The bridge marks the boundary where Columbia River rules change to Umatilla River rules. Anchored boaters and bank anglers also work this area with shrimp or roe fished under a slip bobber or directly on the bottom.

The area known as the county line between lateral mark 70 and lateral mark 64 occasionally produces salmon or steelhead. Even farther downstream, near lateral mark 57, is the Irrigon Fish Hatchery. Cold water from deep wells is used here to raise salmon and steelhead from the eye-up egg stage to the smolt stage. The smolts are then moved to the headwaters of various streams and released for migration to the ocean. The cold water from the hatchery drains into the

This viewing window in the fish ladder on the Washington side of McNary Dam is now closed due to the terrorist threats, but the Oregon window still offers an opportunity to view upstream traffic.

Columbia River in a series of outfalls along the riverbank. This fresh water seems to attract migrating salmon and steelhead and this in turn attracts anglers. You can pull plugs along here near the Oregon shore or anchor up and work Flatfish and Kwikfish.

McNary Dam is equipped with fish ladders on both the Oregon and Washington sides. allowing migrating fish to head on upstream to spawning grounds in the Snake and Clearwater River drainages or up the Columbia River where the Hanford Reach area offers the only free-flowing stretch of river above Bonneville Dam

Directly above McNary Dam there are boat ramps on both shores. This area is popular with boat anglers and bank anglers alike. The off-limits area above the dam is clearly marked by a line of buoys extending across the reservoir. Most boaters pull plugs or drift bobbers along this buoy line. Other boaters work farther upstream to the area marked by a pump house on the Washington shore and a day-use park on the Oregon shore. This entire area is productive. Fish are caught right up against the bank and clear out in the 80-foot water in the middle of the reservoir.

Eileen Theisen with a nice steelhead she caught pulling plugs just above McNary Dam.

Chapter 8

TROLLING

I have reserved this separate chapter for trolling because this tactic is a near-universal method for catching virtually everything that swims in the Columbia River, with the possible exception of sturgeon. The practice of trolling, commonly called "pulling plugs" is extremely popular on this stretch of the river and for good reason: It works.

There is just something about nailing a big fish out on the end of a long line that produces an extra charge of adrenaline. There is no waiting for a nibble or guessing when to set the hook. You don't have to look ruefully at the front half of a nightcrawler knowing that the back half could be residing right now in the mouth of that lunker you just missed.

You're out there motoring along at two or three miles an hour when all of a sudden the rod bends double and the reel starts to sing against the drag. Pandemonium reigns while you try to get the rod out of the holder, throttle back the motor, put down your coffee cup and gulp the rest of your sandwich all at the same time. The only guesswork involved is trying to determine if you have snagged on to a passing locomotive, or, just maybe, you've got yourself a lunker walleye. They do feel much the same.

In this context the term "plug" is just another term to describe crankbaits. Pulling plugs is an effective tactic for salmon, steelhead, walleye, and bass. Lesser species, including catfish, northern pikeminnow, carp, and yellow perch will occasionally hit a trolled plug, although perch are more likely to hit a lure that has been sweetened with a

The five-pound walleye and three-pound smallmouth each hit separate Hawg Boss plugs simultaneously.

nightcrawler. Tactics vary slightly from species to species, but one of the attractive qualities about pulling plugs is that in season you can troll for all four of the major game fish at the same time. I mentioned earlier that fishing for salmon and steelhead can be described as hours and hours of boredom punctuated by a few minutes of sheer pandemonium. Pulling plugs is one way to alleviate that boredom. I will often hit a salmon or steelhead hole for an hour or two. Then when I start to get bored I can move over to one of my favorite walleye or bass hot spots and catch a few fish. Sometimes you don't have to move far. The Columbia outside the mouth of the Umatilla River is a good place for multi-species fishing in the fall of the year. Likewise, you can troll along the Irrigon hatchery looking for a salmon or steelhead and if you fail to find one you can simply move out a little farther toward lateral mark 57 or over by the

Eileen Theisen demonstrates that even carp will sometimes grab a plug.

Channel catfish will occasionally hit a plug being pulled for walleye or bass.

Yellow perch will sometimes hit a plug, but are more likely to hit something with a nightcrawler on it, such as this Northland Whistler Jig.

entrance to Paterson Slough or up to lateral mark 59 and pick up a few bass and maybe a walleye or two. For a dedicated angler it just doesn't get much better than this.

TACKLE

Successful trolling requires selection of the right kind of tackle. You don't have to buy top-of-the-line equipment but neither should you scrimp on mediocre gear. I can't afford to buy separate gear for each kind of fish, so I put together a multi-purpose package that works well for bass, walleye, salmon or steelhead. For what it is worth, here is what I use on a day-to-day basis:

REELS

Shimano Bantam 1500LC line counter or Ambassadeur 6500C3 or 5600CB reels. These are round level wind reels with ample line capacity. They are small enough to fit comfortably in your hand, but beefy enough to handle a salmon or steelhead. The line counter is handy for trolling because it lets you put out exactly the same amount of line each time. With the Ambassadeur or other reels lacking a line counter you can still get pretty close each time by "counting passes".

To do this you need to know how much line comes off the spool each time the line traverses across the spool. Simply position the line up against one side of the spool. Mark the line at the tip of the rod. Then pull line off the reel until the line has moved across the spool and is up against the other side of the spool. Measure how much line came off at that point. For example, my Ambassadeur 6500C3 lets out about 10 feet of line with each pass across the spool. If I want to let out 200 feet of line I simply count 20 passes as the line is coming off the spool.

RODS

Lamiglas G 1330-T Hot Shot Magnum graphite rod. This is an 8-foot single-piece rod rated for lines from 10-20-pound test and lures weighing 3/8 to 2 ounces. It has a straight 14"

TROLLING

Just a few of the many plugs that have proven to be good producers. Clockwise starting from the left: Firetiger Wiggle Wart, Purple Metallic Hawg Boss Super Toad, Purple Half-Ounce Hot Lips, Quarter-Ounce Hot Lips Grape Ape, Black with Sparkle Hawg Boss Super Toad, Red Craw Hawg Boss Super Toad, Green Craw Hawg Boss Super Toad, Quarter-Ounce Hot Lips Reba, Red Metallic Hawg Boss Super Toad, Black with Sparkle Wiggle Wart, Silver & Blue Hawg Boss Super Toad.

cork handle that makes it easy to hold while sitting in the boat or to fit into a rod holder. This may be a little more rod than is needed for bass and walleye, but it works well and has enough backbone for salmon and steelhead. The eight-foot length is handy for keeping the line out from the boat and away from entanglement in the motor.

LINE

For line I prefer one of the non-stretch superlines like Fireline, PowerPro or Spiderwire. For the past several years I have been using 14-pound-test Fireline with excellent results. This line has a small diameter equivalent of 6-pound monofilament yet is strong enough to handle any fish likely to come along. Recent experimentation with the new Spiderwire Stealth superline is promising. I've been trolling with the 20 pound test and results are similar to Fireline. Fireline tends to get a little fuzzy with wear although it still retains most of its strength even after it starts to fray. The Spiderwire Stealth seems to be more resistant to fraying with wear. The bottom line is you can't go wrong with either choice of line.

The lack of stretch makes superlines especially desirable for trolling because that enables you to feel what is going on with the plug even with 200 feet of line out. You can tell when the plug hits bottom, when it thumps a rock, or more importantly when it picks up a weed and stops working properly. Knowing this you can reel the plug in and clear the debris. With monofilament line there is a good chance you would never know the plug has stopped working. It is essential that the plug stay clear of debris. You are not likely to catch anything if you are dragging a weed around the river.

Superline is expensive compared to monofilament, but there are ways to minimize the expense. One way is to fill the spool partially with a less expensive line like braided Dacron or monofilament. You can then tie on 150 yards of superline to finish filling the spool and still have reasonable confidence you won't get spooled by a big fish.

Most of the wear on line occurs on the first 50 or 60 yards. You can get maximum mileage from superline by swapping the line end for end when it starts to get faded and fuzzy. This puts the worn part of the line deep on the spool where it is not likely to ever see the light of day. Just be sure to do this while the line still retains most of its tensile strength. Then in the unlikely event that a big fish takes the line out to the backing you won't lose your prize.

SNAPS AND KNOTS

Tie a Duo-Lock snap to the end of the line and snap it directly onto the eye of the plug. Most manufacturers recommend against using a swivel in addition to the snap. I recommend using a Palomar knot for attaching the snap or any other terminal tackle to the end of a line. The Palomar is one of the strongest knots available. In situations where the Palomar is not convenient then I recommend the Trilene knot. The double UNI-Knot is my knot of choice for joining two lines together. With these three knots you can handle almost any situation that comes along and feel confident that you are not going to lose fish because of a poor or weak knot. If you haven't learned these three knots it is well worth your effort to do so. You can find illustrations on how to tie them on many of the packages in which the line is sold.

PLUGS

There is a mind-boggling assortment of plugs to choose from, so I will only mention a few here that I know to be good producers. Fortunately, many of these will catch all four major game species, salmon, steelhead, walleye, and bass.

Your choice of plug will be determined in large part by the depth of water that you are targeting. With a relatively small number of the right plugs you can work depths ranging from 10 feet to 30 feet without adding any weight to the plug. Below 30 feet you may have to resort to other tactics or figure out some way to weight the plug for added depth. I generally switch to bottom walkers, jigs, or blades when I need to go below 30 feet.

Please note that the depths mentioned in the succeeding paragraphs are approximations and will vary depending on choice of lines and trolling methods. I've generally been able to reach these depths when using 14-pound Fireline with 200 feet of line out and trolling upstream against the current at 2-3 mph. Maximum depth is also heavily dependent on tuning. A well-tuned plug is essential for deep diving. See Chapter 9 for tips on tuning plugs.

SHALLOW RUNNERS

Smallmouth bass often hang around in shallow

Eileen Theisen got this seven-pound, 27-inch walleye on a Hawg Boss Super Toad in green crawfish pattern.

This four-pound walleye hit the Hawg Boss Super Toad in black with sparkle pattern.

Technical Sergeant Paul Theisen, USAF, on leave from Misawa AB, Japan, with his family; got this nice smallmouth pulling a Hawg Boss Super Toad in red crawfish pattern.

water. On some occasions even walleye will be found shallow. A couple good plugs for working waters under 10 feet are the Rapala Shad Rap, size 5 or 7, by Rapala (www.rapala.com) and the Wally Diver, size CD5 or CD6, by Cotton Cordell Lures (www.lurenet.com).

MEDIUM RUNNERS

For depths ranging from 10 to 20 feet there are many good choices. These include the Wiggle Wart by Storm (www.stormlures.com), the Hot Lips quarter-ounce by Luhr-Jensen (www.luhrjensen.com), and the Hawg Boss Super Toad by Worden Lures (www.yakimabait.com). The Hawg Boss Super Toad II has a smaller bill for working the upper end of this range. The Super Toad dives deeper than the Super Toad II.

The Storm company recently redesigned their line of Wiggle Warts. Some local anglers were partial to the older style even though the newer ones look similar. Another brand gaining popularity in this region is being marketed by Brad's B.S. Fish Tales, www.BSFishTales.com. They are marketing a line of plugs called Wee Wigglers, Wigglers and Magnum Wigglers that are virtually identical to the older line of Storm Wiggle Warts.

DEEP RUNNERS

For depths greater than 20 feet try the Magnum Wiggle Wart, or the half-ounce Hot Lips. A well-tuned Hawg Boss

Super Toad also will often go below 20 feet. Luhr-Jensen offers the Power Dive and the 3/4-ounce Hot Lips for depths below 25 feet.

PATTERNS

Here we enter a murky area where there are almost as many opinions as there are anglers to voice them. This perhaps accounts for the mind-boggling assortment of colors and styles found on tackle racks. Nevertheless, I'll step out on a limb here and mention some patterns that have worked well for me. Your mileage may vary.

BLACK WITH SPARKLE - All of the major tackle makers offer this pattern. It is the closest thing to a universal lure that I can think of. It is one of my favorite go-to lures when no clear favorite emerges. I've caught bass, walleye, steelhead, catfish, carp, northern pikeminnow and perhaps others that escape my memory on this pattern. It doesn't look like anything that swims in nature, so I have no idea why it works. I just know it does work and it produces a lot of catches over time. The Hawg Boss Super Toad is also available with a variant of this pattern that has white stripes top and bottom. That is a good producer as well.

CRAWFISH - A popular pattern for bass and walleye and to a lesser extent other species. Available in various shades of red, green, or brown. All worth a try at one time or another.

RED METALLIC - With or without sparkles this is a popular pattern for salmon and steelhead and will catch bass and walleye as well.

PURPLE METALLIC - Like red, this comes with or without sparkles and will catch most anything. My biggest salmon, a 25-pound chinook, came on a purple metallic with sparkle quarter-ounce Hot Lips known locally as the Grape Ape just outside the mouth of the Umatilla River. That same season my wife Eileen caught a four-pound smallmouth on the same lure down by the Irrigon fish hatchery.

SILVER AND BLUE - A good pattern for bass and walleye, and also known to produce steelhead.

HOT PINK AND BRIGHT ORANGE - Popular for salmon and steelhead. Often dressed up with herringbone stripes.

FIRETIGER - A good multi-species pattern offered by all tackle makers. A good one to try when nothing else seems to be producing.

OTHERS TO CONSIDER - If you still have some room in your tackle box, toss in a few of these: Clearwater Flash, Perch, Chartreuse and Green, Shad, Pink Metallic, or White.

TACTICS

Most anglers pull plugs upstream against the current, but this is not a hard and fast rule. You can also hit fish pulling downstream. For bass and walleye pick out a promising breakline. If you don't have a definite depth determined I'd

Nancy Ketterling of Pasco, Washington, got her best ever walleye, this 9.5-pound, 28-inch lunker, pulling a black Hawg Boss Super Toad with sparkle and white stripe.

recommend working the 18- to 25-foot range for starters. If that doesn't produce fish then try shallower or deeper, but for most times of the year you can find fish in that range. Let out 150 to 200 feet of line and troll at a pretty good clip. These fish can easily manage to chase down a lure traveling at 3 or 4 mph. I generally start at 2-3 mph and vary the speed up or down from there.

Troll along the breakline with an eye to the sonar so that you maintain a depth consistent with the plug. Watch the action on your rod tip to make sure the plug is working properly. If the action on the rod tip stops it is likely you have picked up a weed. Sometimes a vigorous jerk on the rod will free the debris. Other times you will need to reel in the plug and clear the debris. In any event, when the action quits you are no longer fishing, but just wasting your time, as it is very unlikely any fish will hit a plug that is fouled with a weed.

For walleye especially it is essential that you keep the plug ticking along on the bottom at frequent intervals. For other species this may not be as critical, but it doesn't do any harm to bounce the bottom as well. I think the action of the plug whacking and rebounding off the rocks on the bottom tends to trigger fish into striking. For this reason you need to match the plug to the depth to assure that you can reach the bottom.

TROLLING

The Haug Boss Super Toad in silver and blue proved too much for this nice smallmouth.

Paul Theisen got this nice smallmouth on a Haug Boss Super Toad in the metallic purple pattern.

Speed changes also seem to trigger strikes. Smallmouth bass will often hit a plug after you stop the boat and start reeling in the plug for another pass. Another way to vary the speed of the plug is to troll in an S-shaped pattern. The plug on the outside of the turn will speed up and the one on the inside will slow down as you do this. This little change in speed will often trigger a strike. Moving the boat like this also will keep the plug from passing directly under the path of the boat at least part of the time.

When you do get a strike you will know it instantly. The speed of the boat is generally fast enough that you will get a good hookset without any special effort on your part. The

exception to this may be when you are trolling slowly for salmon or steelhead, in which case you should probably set the hook.

Be prepared to lose a few plugs. With the plug thumping the bottom it is inevitable that you will get a few snags, but it doesn't happen as often as you might think. When you do hit a snag there is a good chance you can still get the plug back. One of the first actions to take when you hit a snag is to let some slack in the line. Often the plug will float free of its own accord. Don't be too quick to slacken the line though because a lunker walleye often feels like a snag for the first few seconds after it hits. Walleye are lethargic fighters anyway and it usually takes a few seconds after the hookup to feel some head shaking, when you know for sure it's a fish and not a snag.

Once you've determined that you are snagged and not hooked up on a fish, turn the boat around and follow the line downstream until you are well below the snag before you put heavy pressure on the line. The plug will often come free then. Pulling upstream against a snag will increase the chance of breaking the line.

Backtrolling is an effective technique for steelhead. To do this, position the boat upstream from the hole you are targeting and adjust the speed of the boat so that it is essentially standing still in relation to the shore or even sliding backwards slightly. The plug will be working in the current. Then you can maneuver the boat back and forth so that the plug works laterally back and forth across the hole. This technique is popular in the area around the green can near the I-82 bridge. The current is usually swift enough there to put good action on a plug while the boat remains stationary.

Trolling is a popular tactic directly above McNary Dam for salmon and steelhead. You probably don't need as much line out here because you won't be bumping bottom most of the time anyway. Many anglers let out less than 100 feet. The typical speed here is much slower, however, than for walleye and bass downstream. Most anglers just idle down the kicker motor as slow as it will go. Some use the electric motor to go even slower. The majority of the boaters troll back and forth across the reservoir near the buoy line between Washington and Oregon shores.

Trolling is a good way to introduce children to the sport of fishing. When they hook a fish they get so excited and reel so fast that you have to rein them in a bit to keep them from winding the fish right up to the tip of the rod.

Eileen Theisen hit this four-pound smallmouth on a quarter-ounce Hot Lips in the purple metallic with sparkle Grape Ape pattern.

Brian Ketterling, 4, of Pasco, Washington, fishing with his father John, got this smallmouth pulling a Hawg Boss Super Toad in the firetiger pattern.

Chapter 9
PLUG TUNING

How many plugs have you got gathering dust in the bottom of your tackle box because they won't run straight? When your piano falls out of tune you can call a professional, but when your plugs get out of tune you're on your own.

Well-tuned plugs are a vital necessity for successful trolling. Once you have found a good deep-running plug that produces lots of fish, guard it with your life. Don't loan it to your best friend or even your spouse. Often you can recognize a fine plug by its appearance. The bill will be scratched and dented from the constant collisions with rocks on the bottom. The paint on the sides will be worn off from the rubbing of the treble hooks and the teeth marks of fish now residing only in memory. The best plug may be the rattiest looking plug in your tackle box. It's worth its weight in gold.

Generally, manufacturers do a good job of making plugs that run straight right out of the box. Yet, in spite of their best efforts, a fair number will still need tuning.

You'll know a plug needs tuning if it veers to one side or the other. In some cases it will continue running like this, but it won't reach its maximum depth. Other times it will veer off to one side and then pop to the surface. Occasionally a plug will seemingly run fine for awhile and then suddenly pop to the surface.

The tuning procedure is essentially the same for most popular plugs. The only tool you need is a good pair of needlenose pliers. The pliers found on popular multi-tools like the Leatherman will work just fine.

Tuning can be done either from shore or from a boat. Using a boat is more time-consuming, but likely yields better results. Take your boat out on a calm day. It helps if you have a companion who can steer the boat on a straight course while you do the tuning.

Start by tying a Duo-Lock snap without a swivel to the main line. Attach the snap to the eye of the plug. Put the boat in motion at a slow trolling speed and trail the plug in the water alongside the boat while you watch it run. If the plug runs to the right as you look back at it from the boat, take the needlenose pliers and, with the front end of the plug facing you, bend the line attaching eye ever so slightly to the left.

With the plug facing you as shown, bend the line attaching eye ever so slightly in the direction you want the plug to run.

That is to say, with the front end of the plug facing you, bend the eye in the direction you want the plug to run. Be careful not to bend the eye too much. A tiny fraction of an inch can produce a very noticeable effect.

Repeat this procedure until the plug runs straight at slow speed alongside the boat. Then speed the boat to its maximum trolling speed, say 3 or 4 mph. Fine-tune again if necessary. Now you are ready to try the plug under actual trolling conditions.

Seek out a water depth that is a foot or two short of the maximum depth you expect this particular type of plug to run. For example, using 14-pound Fireline, a Wiggle Wart should run deeper than 15 feet, a Hawg Boss Super Toad deeper than 18 feet and a half-ounce Hot Lips deeper than 20 feet.

Let out about 150 feet of line and start trolling at a normal medium to fast speed. The plug should soon find bottom and consistently thump along on the bottom for as long as you care to troll.

If the plug does not find bottom or pops to the top you still have more tuning to do. From this point, tuning can be difficult and is essentially a trial-and-error process. Occasionally you will find a bad actor that just won't run right no matter what you do. I've seen plugs with tiny leaks that allow water in. They run OK for awhile and then go haywire as water seepage changes the weight and balance. The only recourse in a case like this is to discard it or return it for a refund or exchange.

Tuning Flatfish and Kwikfish may be a little easier. The line-attach eye, tail-hook eye and belly eye are generally eye screws. Before bending the line-attach eye, try just aligning it by screwing it in or out until it is lined up with the body. Also align the tail and belly hook eyes parallel with the body. This will probably tune it.

If not, you may have to bend the line-attach eye as above. Remember, though, that these plugs are intended to be trolled very slowly. Don't expect that any amount of tuning will enable them to run fast. When in tune, they just wobble from side-to-side in a rhythmic fashion. Some manufacturers supply specific tuning instructions in the package with their plugs.

This whole routine may seem like a lot of trouble, and it is, but a well-tuned plug will put fish in the boat when those dust collectors won't, especially when the bite is slow.

A simpler alternate procedure is to try tuning the plugs from shore. It won't simulate the trolling routine as well, but will still spot plugs badly out of tune. Just attach the plug to a casting or spinning rod, cast the plug into water of a sufficient depth and retrieve it at a rapid clip. If it veers to one side when retrieving, adjust it as described above until it retrieves in a straight line.

Chapter 10

RIVER CHARTS

River charts in this book are taken from the Evergreen Pacific Cruising Atlas with the permission of Evergreen Pacific Publishing, Ltd. This 11" x 17", spiral-bound river atlas contains large-scale reproductions of NOAA charts for the Columbia River from its mouth to the Tri-Cities, the Snake River from the Tri-Cities to Lewiston, Idaho, and the Willamette River from Portland to Newberg. Major facilities (& their services) along these rivers are indicated on the charts. A special chart of dangerous bar areas for the mouth of the Columbia River is included, along with charts of Ilwaco Harbor, Bonneville Dam, Hood River, The Dalles, and John Day River. Also included are NOAA coastal charts extending north to Destruction Island, WA, & south to Yaquina Head, the last edition of Army Corps charts of the Upper Snake River (to Hells Canyon Dam), a guide to the Hanford Reach, a lower Snake River Recreational guide, and the United States Coast Pilot for the Columbia, Willamette, & Snake Rivers. Visit Evergreen Pacific Publishing's web site at www.evergreenpacific.com.

These charts are an invaluable tool for anyone desiring to learn more about getting around on the river. All the lateral marks described in this book are shown on these charts. The charts also illustrate in topographic form what the bottom of the river looks like. Water depths are depicted by contour lines. Copies of the chart book are available locally in Hermiston.

Points of interest described in the text of this book are annotated in blue on the charts included in this chapter.

Chart taken from the *Evergreen Pacific River Cruising Atlas* with the permission of the publisher. Visit their web site at www.evergreenpacific.com

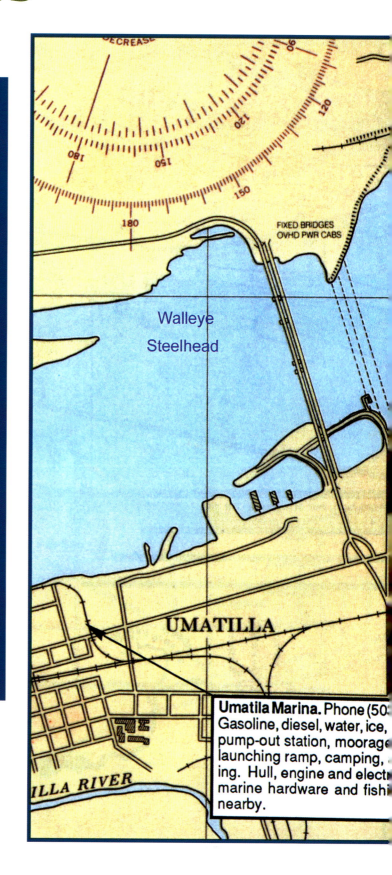

Walleye
Steelhead

FIXED BRIDGES
OVHD PWR CABS

UMATILLA

ILLA RIVER

Umatila Marina. Phone (50: Gasoline, diesel, water, ice, pump-out station, moorage launching ramp, camping, ing. Hull, engine and elect marine hardware and fishi nearby.

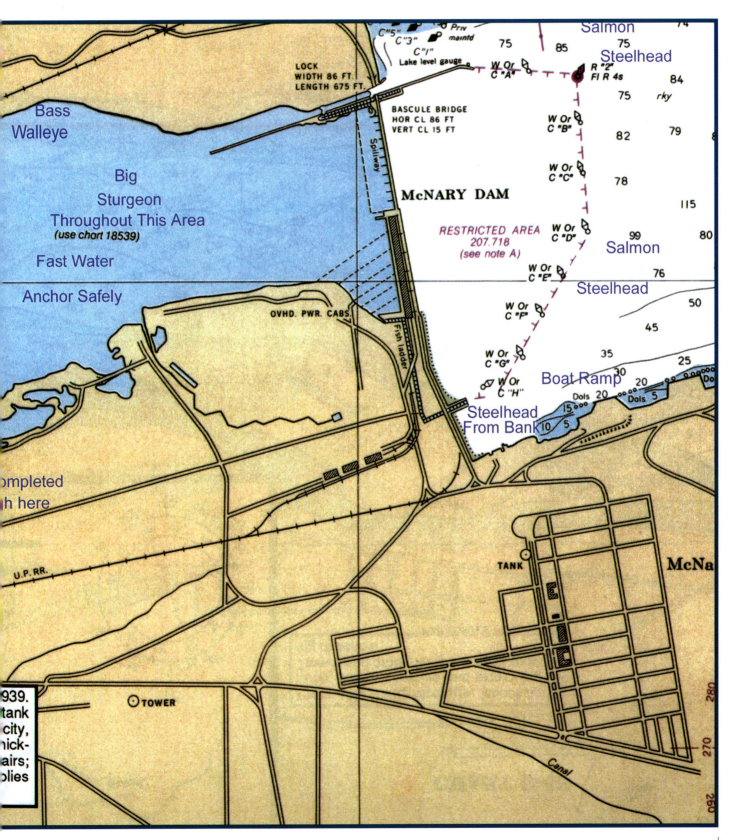

Bass

Walleye

Big

Sturgeon

Throughout This Area

(use chart 18539)

Fast Water

Anchor Safely

mpleted

h here

U.P. RR.

939.

tank

city,

ick-

airs;

lies

⊙ TOWER

LOCK
WIDTH 86 FT.
LENGTH 675 FT.

C"5"   Priv
C"3"   maintd
C"1"
Lake level gauge

BASCULE BRIDGE
HOR CL 86 FT
VERT CL 15 FT

Spillway

McNARY DAM

RESTRICTED AREA
207.718
(see note A)

OVHD. PWR. CABS.

Fish ladder

Salmon
Steelhead

75   85   75

W Or
C "A"

R "2"
Fl R 4s   84

75   rky

W Or
C "B"   82   79

W Or
C "C"   78

115

W Or
C "D"   99   80

Salmon

W Or
C "E"   76

Steelhead

W Or
C "F"   50

45

W Or
C "G"   35   25

30
W Or   Boat Ramp
C "H"   20

Dols 20   Dols 5

Steelhead   15
From Bank   10   5

TANK   McNa

Canal

280

270

260

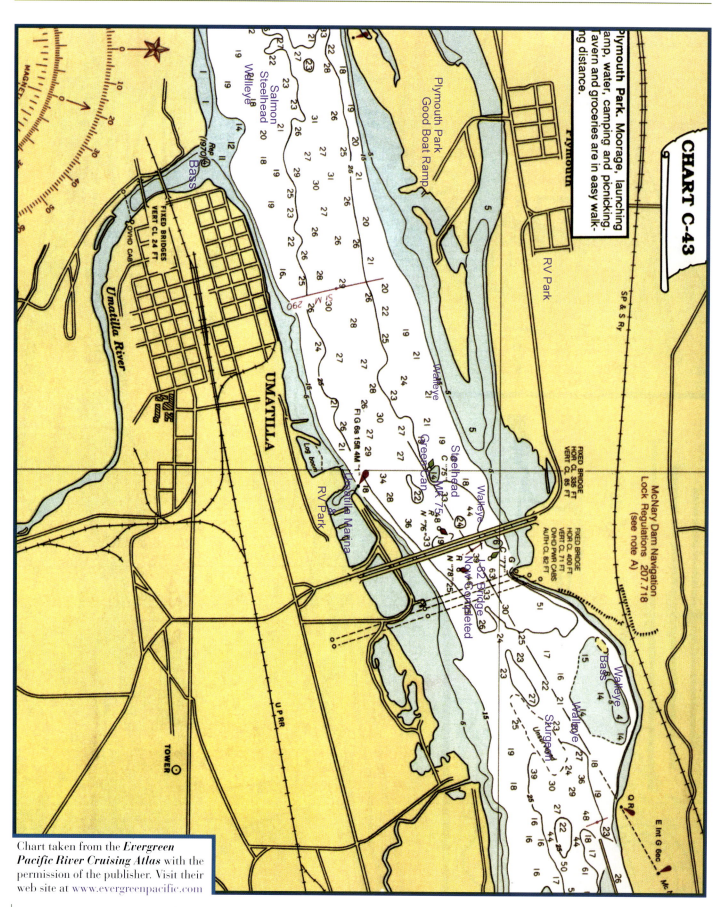

CHART C-43

Plymouth Park. Moorage, launching ramp, water, camping and picnicking. Tavern and groceries are in easy walking distance.

Plymouth Park
Good Boat Ramp

Plymouth

RV Park

McNary Dam Navigation Lock Regulations 207.718 (see note A)

FIXED BRIDGE
HOR CL 335 FT
VERT CL 85 FT

FIXED BRIDGE
HOR CL 400 FT
VERT CL 71 FT
OVHD PWR CABS
AUTH CL 82 FT

FIXED BRIDGES
VERT CL 24 FT

I-82 Bridge
Now Completed

UMATILLA

Umatilla River

Umatilla Marina

RV Park

Log boom

Salmon
Steelhead
Walleye

Walleye

Walleye

Steelhead

Green Can

Bass

Walleye

Sturgeon

Bass

Walleye

TOWER

U P R R

SP & S Ry

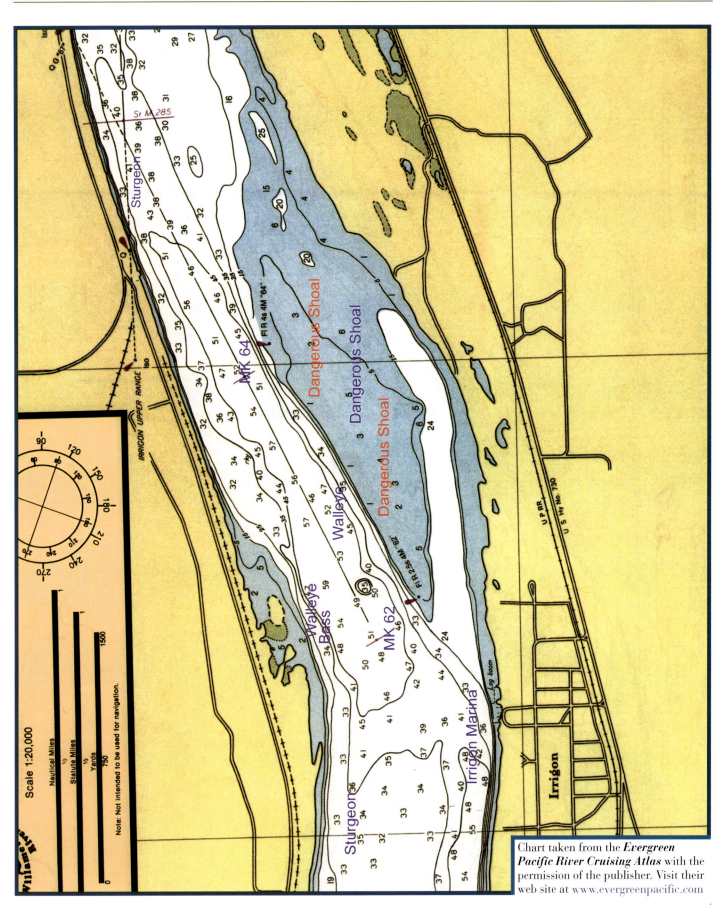

Scale 1:20,000

Nautical Miles

½

Statute Miles

½

Yards

750

Note: Not intended to be used for navigation.

Willamette River

IRRIGON UPPER RANGE

St M 285

Sturgeon

MK 64

F1 R 4s 4M "64"

Dangerous Shoal

Dangerous Shoal

Dangerous Shoal

Dangerous Shoal

Walleye

Walleye
Bass

MK 62

F1 R 2.5s 4M "62"

Irrigon Marina

Sturgeon

Sturgeon

Log boom

U P RR

U S Hy No. 730

Irrigon

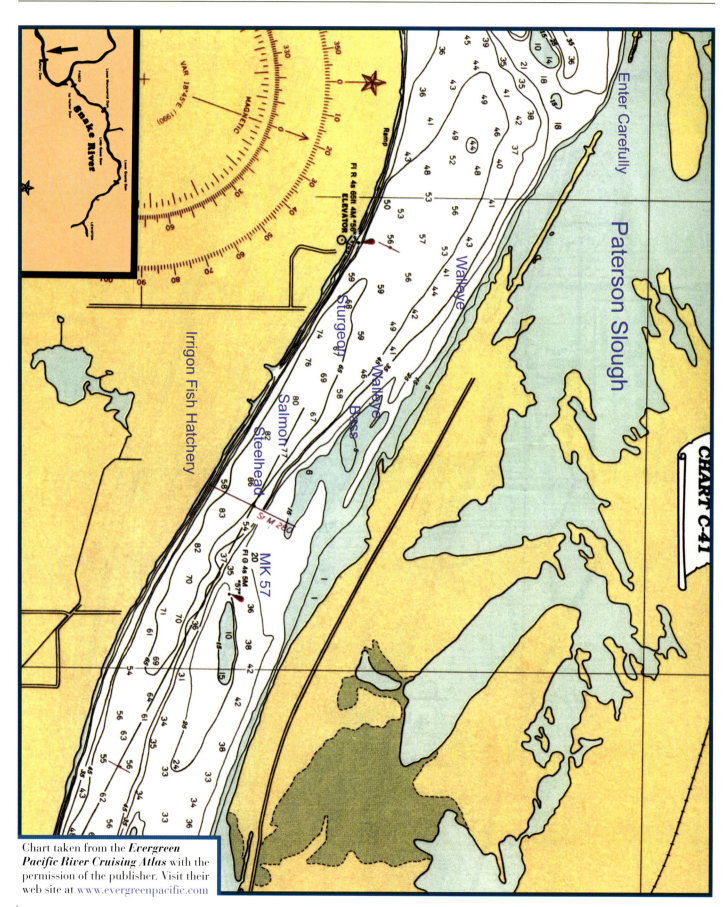

Chart taken from the *Evergreen Pacific River Cruising Atlas* with the permission of the publisher. Visit their web site at www.evergreenpacific.com

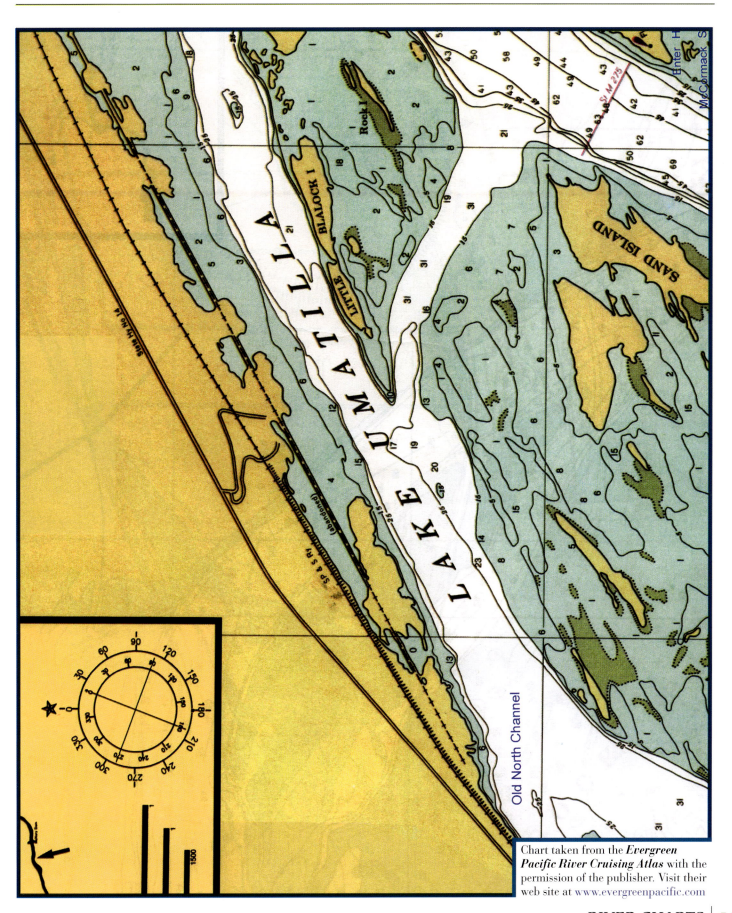

LAKE UMATILLA

BLALOCK I

LITTLE

Rock I

SAND ISLAND

Old North Channel

S/ M 275

Enter H

McCormack S

(abandoned)

SP & S Ry

SP & S Ry No 14

Chart taken from the *Evergreen Pacific River Cruising Atlas* with the permission of the publisher. Visit their web site at www.evergreenpacific.com

RIVER CHARTS

Chart taken from the **Evergreen Pacific River Cruising Atlas** with the permission of the publisher. Visit their web site at www.evergreenpacific.com

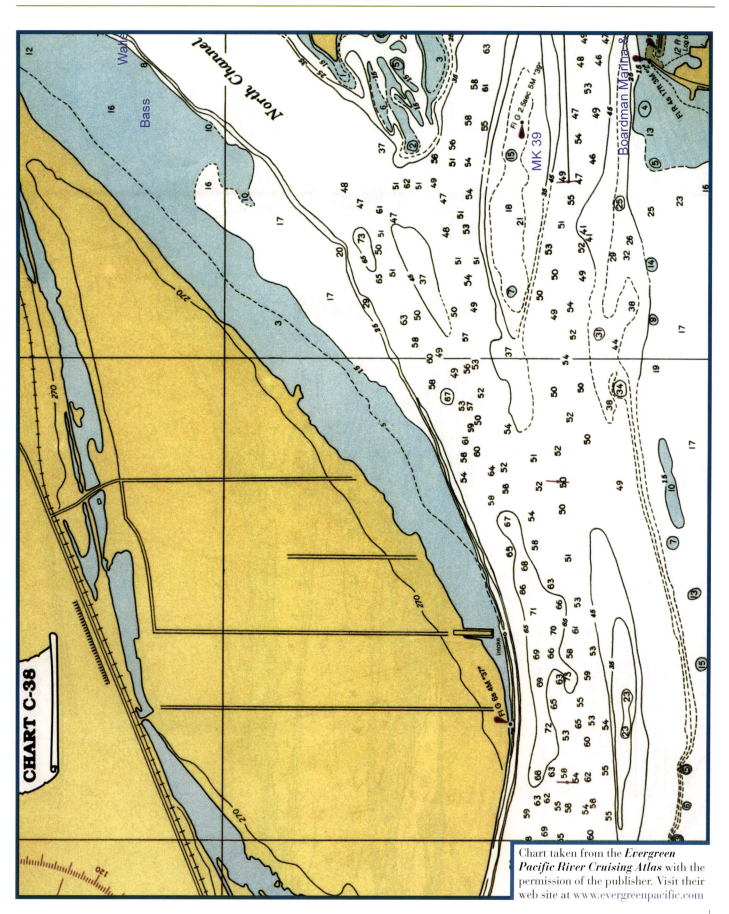

CHART C-38

North Channel

Bass

Watt

Boardman Marina &

MK 39

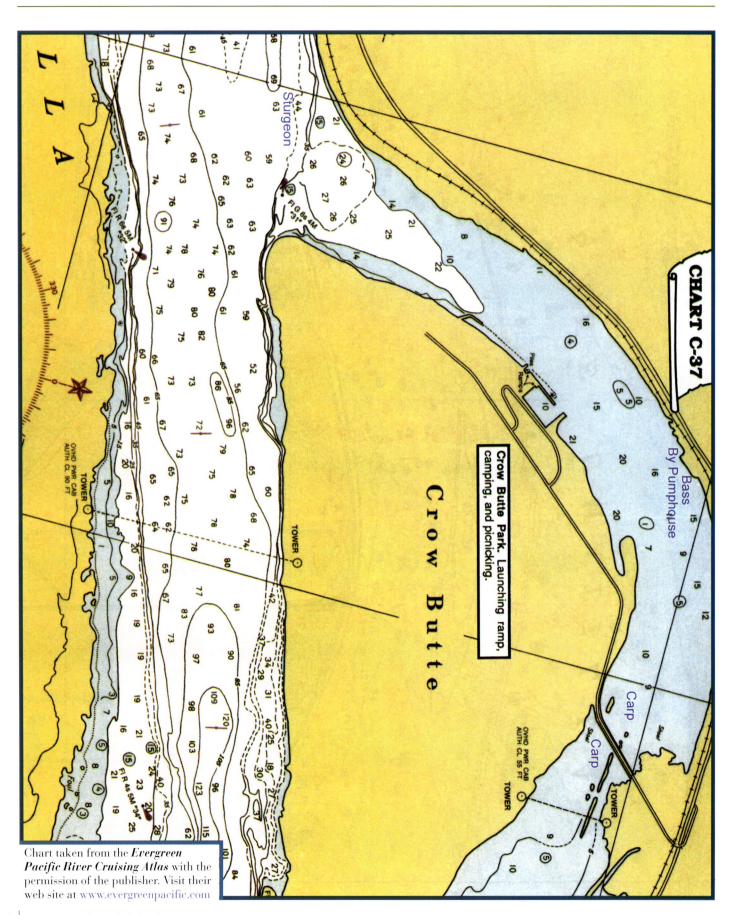

CHART C-37

Bass
By Pumphouse

Carp

Carp

Crow Butte Park. Launching ramp, camping, and picnicking.

Crow Butte

Sturgeon

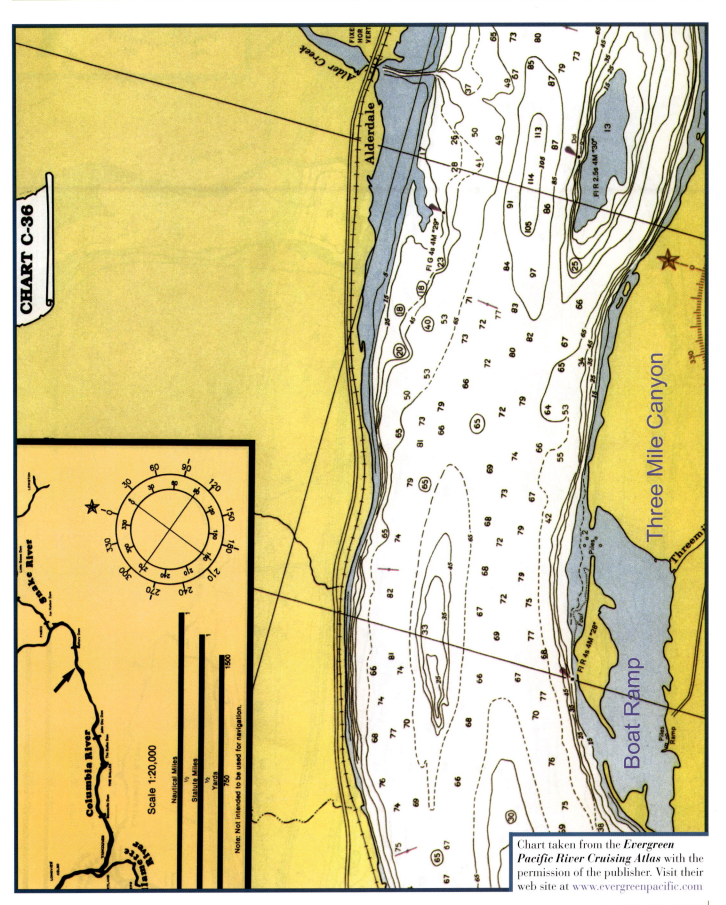

CHART C-36

Scale 1:20,000

Nautical Miles
Statute Miles
Yards

Note: Not intended to be used for navigation.

Columbia River

Snake River

Willamette River

Alder Creek

Alderdale

Three Mile Canyon

Boat Ramp

Fl R 2.5s 4M "30"

Fl G 4s 4M "29"

Fl R 4s 4M "28"

Fl R 4s 4M "26"

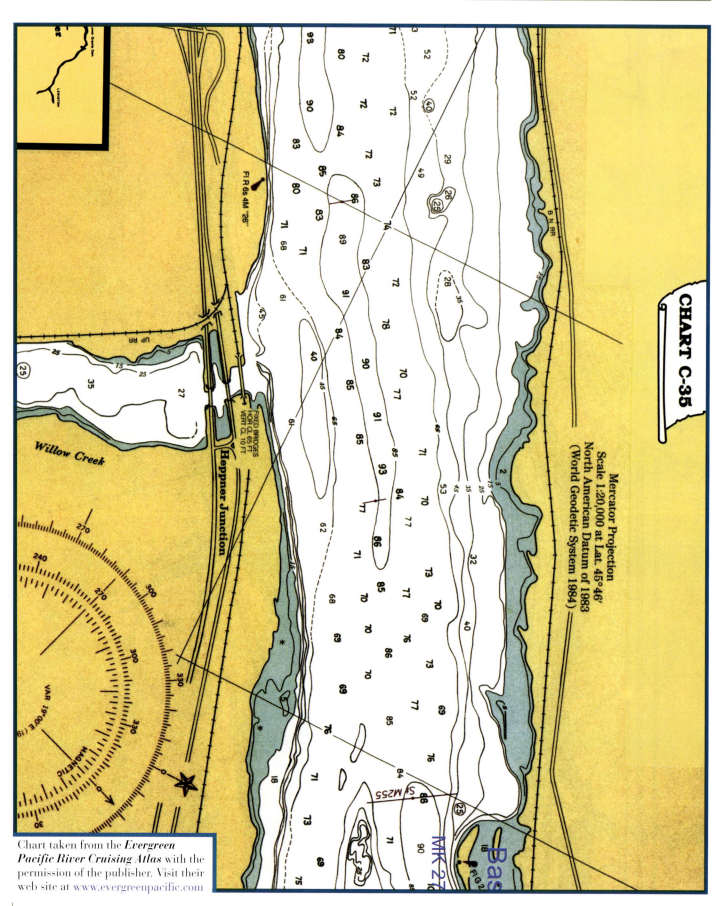

CHART C-35

Mercator Projection
Scale 1:20,000 at Lat. 45°46'
North American Datum of 1983
(World Geodetic System 1984)

Willow Creek

Heppner Junction

FIXED BRIDGES
HOR CL 65 FT
VERT CL 10 FT

Fl R 6s 4M "26"

UP RR

B N RR

Bas

MK 27

FIG 2

S M255

Chapter 11

TERMINAL TACKLE

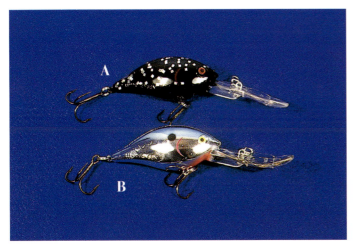

A. *Hot Lips, black with sparkle.*
B. *Hot Lips, silver and blue.*

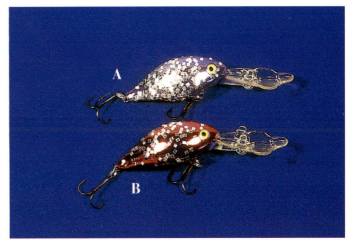

A. *Hot Lips, grape ape.*
B. *Hot Lips, reba.*

Kwikfish.

Wiggle Wart, firetiger.

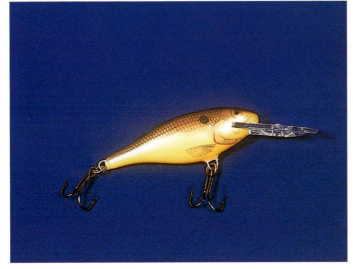

Rapala Shad Rap, gold.

Wally Diver, green and chartreuse.

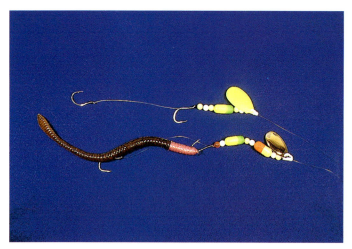

Typical Spinner/worm harnesses.

Typical Spinner/worm harnesses.

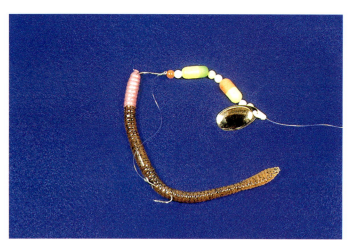

Typical Spinner/worm harnesses.

Typical lead-head jig and twin-tail plastic grub.

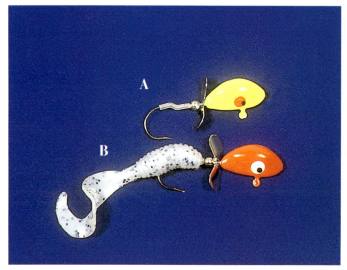

A. *Northland whistler jigs,* **B.** *Plastic grub.*

Typical hand-crafted quarter-ounce spinners.

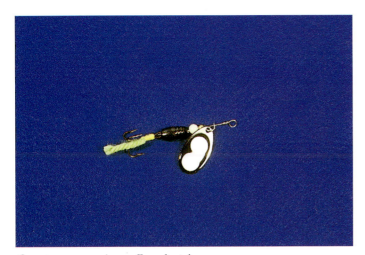

Quarter-ounce spinner, French style.

Quarter-ounce spinner, in-line style.

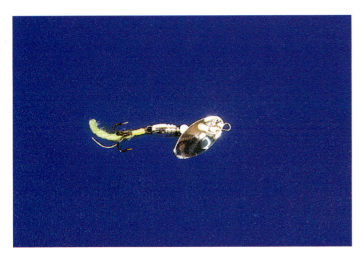

Quarter-ounce spinner, in-line style.

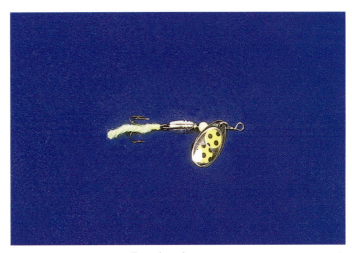

Quarter-ounce spinner, French style.

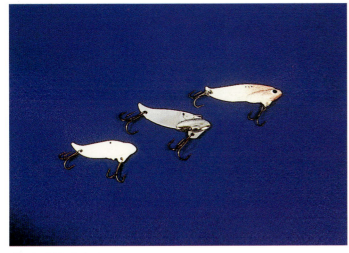

Typical blade baits.

Appendix 1

FACILITIES

Anglers living locally as well as those coming from out of the area are fortunate to have ample facilities for launching their boats, as well as camping facilities for tents and recreational vehicles (RVs). Motels are available in Umatilla, Hermiston, and Boardman.

Directly above McNary Dam on the Oregon side is a good place for boaters and bank anglers alike.

Above McNary Dam (Lake Wallula)

The pool above McNary Dam is called Lake Wallula. There are boat ramps provided by the Army Corps of Engineers directly above McNary Dam on both the Oregon and Washington sides. Launching is free here. On the Oregon side the Corps has provided a handicapped-accessible fishing platform with concrete walkway, railings, benches, and rod holders. Bank anglers do quite well here for steelhead and an occasional bass or catfish.

Below McNary Dam (Lake Umatilla)

This pool is backed up by the John Day Dam and is called Lake Umatilla.

The Umatilla Marina and RV Park is well equipped for boats of almost any size.

UMATILLA MARINA AND RV PARK

Directly below the dam on the Oregon side is the Umatilla Marina and RV Park.

The Umatilla Marina and RV Park is well equipped for boats of almost any size. This park, operated by the Port of Umatilla, offers a marina and boat ramps that can accommodate virtually any size boat. The fuel dock offers both gasoline and diesel fuel. There are transient boat slips available for an extra charge if you want to moor a boat during your stay. A pumpout station is available for boat holding tanks.

The RV park has full hookups including electricity, water, and sewer and can accommodate rigs of all sizes from tents to 40-foot luxury coaches. Sites are level and spacious with room to park a boat and an extra vehicle. Restrooms and showers are provided.

You don't have to be registered at the RV park to use the marina facilities and boat ramps. There is ample parking for tow vehicles and trailers in the marina parking lot. Launching is free here. A fish-cleaning station is provided.

The Umatilla Marina and RV Park is the site of the annual Oregon Governor's Cup Walleye Derby held in September each year. This facility is open year-round.

For reservations or information call (541) 922-3939. The mailing address is 1710 Quincy, P.O. Box 277, Umatilla, OR 97882. Visit their web site at: www.portofumatilla.com

PLYMOUTH PARK

Plymouth Park is directly across the river from Umatilla. To get there just cross the bridge to the Washington side of the river and take the first exit off the freeway onto State Route 14. Turn west and follow the signs to Plymouth.

This park is operated by the Corps of Engineers. The park has 32 RV sites, half with full hookups including electricity, water, and sewer. Restrooms and showers are available. An RV dump site is available. The sites are spacious, attractive, and well shaded by mature trees. You may have to park your boat in an alternate area away from your campsite, depending on the size of your rig and boat.

Nearby, out on an island reached by a causeway, is the day-use area. Here you will find a big swimming beach and picnic area. Also on the island are improved boat ramps and docks. A nominal fee is charged for the day-use area or boat launching if you are not registered in the RV park. No fuel is available here.

Holders of Golden Age or Golden Access Passports qualify for campsites at half price. The park is open from April 1st to October 31st. Reservations can be made by calling 1-877-444-6777 or by checking their web site at www.reserveusa.com. You can reach the park directly by calling (509) 783-1270.

IRRIGON MARINA

About seven miles downriver from Umatilla, on Highway 730, is the town of Irrigon and the Irrigon Marina and Park. Signs directing to the marina are clearly posted on the road as you enter town. Here you will find a small marina and docks able to accommodate average-size fishing vessels.

A small day-use park with restrooms is available here. No fuel or commercial services are provided.

BOARDMAN MARINA AND RV PARK

Just off Interstate 84 west of Irrigon is the town of Boardman. Take the Boardman exit (Exit #164) and follow the signs to the Boardman Marina and RV Park. This park is operated by the Boardman Park and Recreation District.

The park offers 63 full hookup sites with water, sewer, and electricity. Most have 30 amp service and a few have 50 amps.

Park amenities include showers and restrooms, playground, swimming, Laundromat, hiking trail, fish cleaning station, and RV dump. Tent camping is permitted.

The park also features a spacious marina with public boat docks and large improved ramps. You don't have to be registered in the RV park to use the day-use areas or boat ramps. Launching here is free.

This park is the site of the other two Columbia River Circuit walleye tournaments, the Smoker-Craft/Sylvan Spring Classic, held in March, and the High Desert Marine Walleye Derby held in July.

The RV park is open from March 1st until November 1st, except for four sites equipped with heat tape for winter visitors. The boat ramps are open year-round. For reservations or information call (541) 481-7217, or 1-888-481-7217. Visit their web site at: http://www.eoni.com/~parkdu/

THREE-MILE CANYON

Farther west from Boardman on I-84 is the Three-Mile Canyon exit (Exit #151). Here there are multiple facilities. A primitive ramp without a dock is provided for public use, as is a restroom. A deluxe ramp with a dock is available for exclusive use by certain Indian Tribes. The Indian facility also features a restroom, water and camp sites. No fuel or services are available here.

CROW BUTTE PARK

The fate of this beautiful park was in jeopardy when the State of Washington announced in 2002 that it would no longer operate this facility as a state park. Budgetary shortfalls were blamed as the reason. The state's lease was terminated and the park returned to the Army Corps of Engineers. The Corp has announced that they are seeking a concessionaire to operate the park. With any luck, by the time you read this the park should be open to the public again. The park re-opened on August 13, 2003. Reservations can be made by calling (509) 875-2644.

This is mighty good news for anglers. The Crow Butte boat ramp is the only public launch facility on the Washington side for the entire 52-mile stretch of river between Plymouth and Roosevelt.

The rising waters impounded by the John Day Dam turned Crow Butte into an island, now accessible only by a causeway leading from the Washington shore. The park encompasses about 1,300 acres, or approximately half the entire island. The remainder of the island is part of the Umatilla National Wildlife Refuge. With some 25 acres of grass and mature shade trees the park is a welcome green oasis in the otherwise arid landscape.

The park features 50 full-hookup RV sites plus a spacious day-use area. Restrooms and showers are available in both areas. There are improved boat ramps and a boat basin with docks for mooring boats. A swimming beach is also provided.

To reach Crow Butte Park take Washington State Route 14 about 28 miles west from Plymouth. This highway parallels the river all the way to Vancouver. It is designated as a scenic highway and represents a less traveled alternative to Interstate 84 on the other side of the river in Oregon. You will pass through the little town of Paterson along the way. In Paterson there is a sign that reads "no services for 66 miles". What the sign doesn't say is that there in no gas available in Paterson either, unless you count an unattended card facility. You would be well advised to fuel up in Umatilla before heading downriver from Plymouth. While you may not be able to find gas in Paterson, you can find wine. Paterson is home to the Columbia Crest Winery. They have a nice little chateau there with a self-guided tour, plus a tasting room and retail outlet.

The entire cove surrounding the west end of the butte is prime smallmouth habitat. Almost directly across from the boat ramp on the Washington shore there is a pumphouse. Along this area are a number of small islands and many submerged boulders that harbor lots of bass in the spring. This area becomes fouled with milfoil as the season progresses, so it is advisable to get in here early in the season.

If you like to pursue carp the area on both sides of the causeway gets so thick with carp in the spring spawning season that you could almost walk across the water on their backs.

The Irrigon Marina offers boat ramps, mooring slips, docks, restrooms, and a small day-use park.

Appendix 2

OTHER RESOURCES

BAIT, TACKLE, MARINE SUPPLIES, AND INFORMATION
High Desert Marine in Hermiston is a good place to get most anything you need related to fishing on this section of the Columbia River. They carry boats, motors, marine supplies, and the largest selection of tackle in the region. The owner, Rod McKenzie, is active in managing local bass and walleye tournaments. He and all the members of his family are ardent anglers and as a result his store serves as the local clearinghouse for fishing information. High Desert Marine, 30618 Bensel Road, Hermiston, OR 97838. **(541) 567-8419.**

LICENSED PROFESSIONAL FISHING GUIDES
Columbia Basin Guide Service – Bob Roberts, 601 SW Nye Avenue, Pendleton, OR 97801, **(541) 276-0371,** www.columbiafishing.com.

Mid Columbia Guide Service – Craig Turner, 8938 West Quinault Ave., Kennewick, WA 99336.

Hook Setter Guide Service – Ray A. Warren, 1320 SE 9th Street, Hermiston, OR 97838, **(541) 564-7536** or **(541) 379-3921,** email: sturgeonray@eoni.com.

Jason Schultz – Hells Canyon Sport Fishing, **(208) 750-1100,** http://www.hellscanyonsportfishing.com/ Schultz comes over to the area below McNary Dam in March to guide for trophy walleye.

INTERNET WEB SITES
For starters, here is a baker's dozen Internet sites that anglers might find interesting. Links from these sites will lead to dozens or hundreds more depending on your interests.

www.dfw.state.or.us – **Oregon Department of Fish and Wildlife.** Here you will find a weekly fishing report, license and regulations information, statewide guide to fishing opportunities, and more.

www.wa.gov/wdfw – **Washington Department of Fish and Wildlife** – Similar information to the Oregon site. Also a rich source of technical and historic information. This site served as source material for much of this book. Here you will find offered for sale at nominal prices three different spiral-bound identification guides, covering freshwater sport fish, anadromous sport fish, and marine fish. Also offered is a CD entitled "Sport Fish of Washington" compatible with Windows and Macintosh. These are both bargains and I highly recommend them.

www.walleyecentral.com – The Walleye Central site will tell you more about walleye than you ever want to know.

www.streamnet.org – **Streamnet, the Northwest Aquatic Information Network** contains a wealth of information about all the species of fish found in the Pacific Northwest. Streamnet is a cooperative venture of the Pacific Northwest's fish and wildlife agencies and tribes. They provide information and services in support of fish and wildlife programs and other efforts to preserve and restore the region's aquatic resources. Here you will find fish facts, life history profiles, features for kids and other related information.

www.fpc.org – **Fish Passage Center** – If you like to keep track of the species of fish making their way up and down the Columbia and Snake River drainages, take a look at this site, sponsored by the Northwest Power Planning Council. Here you will find weekly or bi-weekly reports of fish passages from March through October.

www.cqs.washington.edu/dart/dart.html - **University of Washington Data Access in Real Time** – Daily fish passage information for the same periods, plus historic information dating back to 1910.

www.psmfc.org/index.html – **Pacific States Marine Fisheries Commission** – Provides links to numerous other sites relating to Pacific Northwest fisheries.

www.cabelas.com and www.basspro.com – If you are of a mind to do some browsing or shopping for the latest in fishing tackle, **Cabela's and Bass Pro Shops** both have online sites where you can check out the merchandise, buy online, or order a new catalog.

www.bassmaster.com – **The Bass Anglers Sportsman Society** is always looking for new members.

www.fieldandstream.com and www.in-fisherman.com – Just two of the many popular magazines for outdoor enthusiasts.

www.WOgameandfish.com – **Washington-Oregon Game & Fish Magazine** – An outdoors magazine tailored to the Pacific Northwest.

Appendix 3

PISCATORIAL PECKING ORDER

How many people would eat a fish that scrounges around on the bottom of a lake or stream eating Velveeta cheese, whole kernel corn, marshmallows, salmon eggs, worms, grasshoppers, rock rollers, crawfish, and a lot of other yucky stuff? The answer is a lot of people would because the fish in question is a trout. Yet many of these same people would refrain from eating a catfish because it is a bottom-dweller. Go figure.

That little example is symptomatic of a phenomenon that seems to prevail in every region of the country. Somehow, by some mysterious process, anglers of every region develop an unwritten hierarchy of fish whereby each fish species is relegated to some spot on a spectrum ranging from fish that are to be admired, revered, and much sought after to those that are to be reviled and tossed up on the bank as just so much trash.

The relative ranking of different species of fish will vary from region to region. In the southeastern region of the United States, for example, the largemouth black bass reigns supreme. In fact, the largemouth bass is quite highly regarded across the country. The 100th anniversary issue of *Outdoor Life* magazine, November, 1999, contains a supplement recapping the magazine's history decade by decade. One highlight from the June, 1964, issue was an assertion by the magazine's then fishing editor, Wynn Davis, that the black bass was America's greatest game fish. This assertion was supported by the announcement that by 1964 more lures were being manufactured for bass fishing than for all other types of fishing combined. In other words, anglers had voted with their wallets.

There is no reason to believe that bass fishing has gotten any less popular since 1964. The Bass Anglers Sportsman Society has grown to more than 600,000 members since their first tournament in 1967.

Here in the Pacific Northwest, the chinook salmon is both literally and figuratively the king. Northwesterners have also voted with their wallets, spending hundreds of millions of dollars every year on salmon-restoration efforts. Steelhead and trout round out the top three in this region.

At the other end of the spectrum is the lowly common carp. Almost no local angler will admit to any admiration for carp. These unfortunate fish are commonly tossed on the bank to rot or feed the seagulls. While it may be true that carp are regarded as a game fish and a delicacy in Europe, they don't get much respect on this side of the Atlantic. Just try to find a local angler who will admit to keeping and cooking a carp.

Logic doesn't always prevail in this ranking process. For example, introduced species, i.e., fish brought in from other regions, are generally less highly regarded than native species. Walleye and smallmouth bass, though highly regarded by many anglers, are two examples of introduced species that find less favor with local fish-and-wildlife authorities.

Interestingly enough, however, there is one native species, the northern pikeminnow, formerly called northern squawfish, that ranks even lower than introduced species. The northern pikeminnow, though native to these waters, is looked upon with such disfavor that it carries a bounty on its head. That's because it shows a propensity to eat little salmon and steelhead that define the image of the Pacific Northwest.

Somewhere between the two extremes are found the rest of the inhabitants of our local waters. Walleye are ranked by many right up there close to salmon and steelhead in spite of the fact that they are an introduced species. That may be because walleye are perhaps the best table fare to be found in fresh water. Maybe it's just the walleye image. Those big wall-eyes and sharp teeth certainly conjure up an image of the ultimate predator. Size is a factor. Walleye in this region often grow to 16 pounds or more and five-pounders are common.

Walleye are certainly not admired for their fighting ability. They never go airborne and generally just come quietly to the boat, at least until they see the net. Then, one or two quick dives toward the bottom and they are ready to give up.

Size is apparently not the defining criterion. If that were the case, sturgeon would go right to the top of the list. Nothing around here compares in size to the local white sturgeon. Yet, these magnificent fish get only a mediocre following from a relatively small part of the angling public. This in spite of the fact that their fighting ability often takes them all over the river and sometimes airborne before they come to the boat.

Smallmouth bass may be victims of the old adage "familiarity breeds contempt". Among the most numerous and readily available game fish in our area, these scrappy little contenders are second to none when it comes to just plain gutsy, aggressive, even outrageous behavior.

Smallies will attack a wide range of lures with reckless abandon. A recent peek at the stomach contents of a smallmouth revealed an entire clam, shell and all, a minnow about four inches long, and a crawfish about three inches long. In spite of this, that fish attacked a plug about four inches long. It is not uncommon for them to follow your lure until it's almost to the side of the boat and smack it just about the time you are ready to pull it out of the water for another cast.

There is a group of fish, often called panfish, somewhere in the middle of the spectrum. These fish include the likes of crappies, bluegills, and perch. Generally small in size, they are not the stuff of tournaments, macho bragging rights, or mounts hanging on the wall, yet they provide a tremendous amount of family enjoyment, especially for children. These fish have the advantage that they are plentiful in numbers, relatively easy to catch, and, when large enough, are tasty in the frying pan.

Catfish are an underrated game fish. They will fight all the way to the boat. But, let's face it, they are ugly. Most people either love 'em or hate 'em. Regarded by many as a deep-fried delicacy, especially in the Southeast, there are others who won't even taste them because of their image.

Rounding out the lower end of the spectrum are such fish as whitefish, shad, sculpins, and suckers. Regarded mostly as nuisance fish, some of them do have their proponents. Shad are often pursued as fun to catch, but not much else. They are used as sturgeon bait. Too full of bones for typical cooking methods, some people can them so that the bones will be soft and edible. Whitefish are edible but not popular. Sculpins serve as a forage fish for larger fish and suckers are ranked along with carp as candidates for the seagulls on the bank.

So there you have it, the Pacific Northwest freshwater ranking spectrum: at the top are found the coldwater native species, salmon, steelhead, and trout. Then the larger warmwater-introduced species including walleye, largemouth bass, and smallmouth bass. On a par with these would be the native white sturgeon. Near the middle of the spectrum would be found the panfish. Toward the lower middle would be catfish. Proceeding downward would be found shad, whitefish, and sculpins, and on the bottom of the heap the lowly carp and sucker. A special kind of trash fish, the native northern pikeminnow shares the bottom of the pile with carp and suckers, but carries a special status, namely, you can get paid for catching them.

These are just my opinions and are not based on any kind of scientific research.

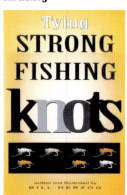

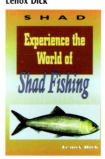

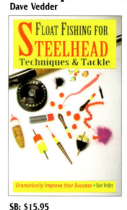